Contents

Foreword

Like wild animals, words are always trying to run away from me, and with my net I chase after them, hoping to catch just the right ones. After thirty years of corralling words, I have learned that these scratchings on paper do some things very well, and some things not so well.

On a trip to Lebanon in 1998, I met a woman who said she had read my book *Disappointment with God* during the Lebanese civil war. She kept it in a basement bomb shelter. When the artillery fire intensified around her high-rise apartment building, she would make her way with a flash-light down the darkened stairway, light a candle, and read my book. I cannot describe how humbling it was for me to hear that, at a moment when Christians were dying for their faith, when the most beautiful city of the Middle East was being reduced to rubble, at that moment words I wrote from my apartment in Chicago somehow brought her comfort.

As I reflect on my own pilgrimage, I realize that I probably became a writer because as a reader I had experienced this same long-distance power. For me, words opened chinks of light that became a window to another world. I became a writer, I now believe, because I saw that spoiled words could be reclaimed. I saw that writing could penetrate into the crevices, bringing spiritual oxygen to people trapped in air-tight boxes. I saw that when God conveyed to us the essence of his self-expression, God called it the Word, the Logos.

The very power of words, however, makes them vulnerable to a kind of deception. Every writer who touches on spirituality can identify with Thomas Merton's concern that his books expressed the spiritual life so confidently and surely when actually he was plagued by insecurities, doubts, and even terrors.

I often have the impression that the words I write have more lasting value than my life, and I sense that the higher I reach in my writing, the more I misrepresent that disorderly life. It is far easier, I find, to edit words than to edit life. When I get letters from readers telling me how my words have affected them, I want to protest, "Yes, but you don't know me, talk to my wife!" Words grant to the writer of faith a vicarious power that we do not deserve.

All art distorts reality, but words most of all because they reduce a sensory life of sound, smell, sight, and touch to symbols on a page. When I write about my own experience with God, I break it down, reassemble it, then polish the words. What vanishes in the process? After the thirteenth edit, I begin to question what prompted my writing in the first place. Like a chemist who breaks down complex molecules into simple ones, in my reductionism I may destroy the very substance I am hoping to assay.

Why do we do it, we writers? "Of making many books there is no end," sighed the Teacher of Ecclesiastes some three millennia ago. Yet we keep at it, cranking out more and more words, with the potential to bring harm as well as comfort.

I think we do it because we have nothing else to offer than a point of view. Everything I write is colored by my family dysfunctions, my upbringing in Southern fundamentalism, my guarded pilgrimage; indeed, every author represented in this collection sees the world through a unique set of eyes. We can only write with passion about our own experiences, not yours. Somehow my rendering of church, family, and my halting steps toward faith *provokes* something. Walker Percy noted that a novelist reveals what the reader knows but does not know he knows.

Five hundred years ago the Renaissance scholar Pico della Mirandola delivered his famous "Oration on the Dignity of Man," which defined the role of humanity in creation. After God had created the animals, all the essential roles had been filled, but "the Divine Artificer still longed for some creature which might comprehend the meaning of so vast an achievement, which might be moved with love at its beauty and smitten with awe at its grandeur." To contemplate and appreciate all the rest, to reflect on meaning, to share in the power and exuberance of creativity, to revere and to hallow these were the roles reserved for the species made in God's image.

"What am I" asked Merton. "I am myself a word spoken by God." Created in God's image, we can only return an interest on that investment. Somehow God perceives his own creation through us, and in the process we reflect back some glimmer of God's own image. Every writer has only a living point of view, which distinguishes him or her from every other person on this planet. We are called to be stewards of that point of view, and stewards of the extraordinary power of words through which we express it.

We do not have to make wine out of water. Indeed, we cannot. We can only provide the water in our leaky clay vessels. If we do so faithfully, God will make the wine.

Philip Yancey

Lucas on Life

Jeff Lucas

Be prepared to be challenged, provoked and nudged as popular speaker and author Jeff Lucas takes you on a memorable journey through life's ups and downs – pointing out lessons that need to be learnt on the way!

In the introduction Jeff writes, 'Lucas on Life is no collection of wisdom from one deeply profound; no deep musings from an inspiring and learned sage. Rather, I've drawn together a collection of stories and episodes that hopefully will make you laugh, sometimes make you cry and occasionally make you think. I speak as someone who loves God, but messes up constantly.'

Authentic Lifestyle
ISBN: 1–8602.4360–6

Price: £6.99

£4.99 with voucher

First published in 2001 by Authentic Lifestyle
9 Holdom Avenue, Bletchley, Milton Keynes,
MK1 1QP

HOORAY FOR SUE!

'I am really offended!'

If I had a pound coin for every time I've heard a Christian use the 'O' word, I'd weigh a ton. Some believers have a fantastic capacity to be offended. They are the ones everyone else in the church describes as 'prickly', 'sensitive', 'awkward', or 'difficult'. You can always hear the crunch crunch of eggshells being walked on when people get around them. It doesn't take much to irritate them. I met four 'black belt' offended types recently. They were older ladies, and they were so upset with me, that they stomped out of the Sunday evening church meeting, before I'd even started preaching. I had noticed that, five rows back, there was a lot of muttering, sniffing, narrowing of eyes, and then finally the march of the haughty four. So why the quadruple walkout? I later learned that my sin was that I had invited the congregation to take a few pre-sermon moments to say hello to each other. Apparently, this particular church didn't include the saying of hello in its vision statement, hence the huffy puffy walkout. The pastor was a warm-hearted, compassionate shepherd, who was eager to visit the retiring sisters to restore them as lost sheep to the flock. I admire him. I was inclined towards a lamb kebab with heaps of mint sauce. Easily offended people bore me.

Sue is a lady that I bumped into recently, who could have so easily have chosen the offended look: you know, pouting lip, downcast eyes, and woundedness bleeding from every pore. But she didn't go that way. She chose to laugh instead.

Sue was walking into our Sunday morning meeting in Chichester. I was in a hurry and didn't pay any attention to the fact that she was pushing something in front of her as she navigated her way through the oaken double doors. Sue had been pregnant: hugely pregnant. So massive had she become during the past nine months that it was rumoured that Goodyear was sponsoring her confinement. Hurrying in behind her, I glanced, momentarily, at what seemed to be her still considerable girth and the words tumbled out before my brain had time to catch them.

'So then Sue, no baby yet?'

She paused in the doorway, obviously stunned by my rank stupidity.

'Actually Jeff, I had the baby this week. That's why I'm pushing this pram, believe it or not'. Her eyes sparkled with the joy that breaks out when one meets a truly, authentically, stupid person like me. But there was no malice or edge in her voice.

'I'm so sorry Sue ... I mean, er, congratulations, it's just that you still look, so, er ...'

'Big' said Sue, completing my hapless sentence. I frantically searched for some ground of the swallow-me-up-now variety.

'Well, er ... sorry ... well done anyway! He's beautiful!' I gushed; praying to God as I did that the bundle before me was a male.

Sue could have been irritated, galled, or just mildly upset by my stupidity – but she was the reverse. She laughed with me, not at me. And the next time I saw her at church, she asked if I was doing okay. 'I nearly telephoned you that afternoon,' she smiled. 'I was worried that you might have been concerned. You didn't have to be at all.' She could have glared, but she grinned. She gave grace in the face of my mindlessness. Her hobbies don't include being offended.

Hooray for Sue!

SORRY

The man in the seat next to me on the aeroplane was chewing tobacco and spitting the juice in a cup. I'm a tolerant enough person, but as another shot of yellow stained saliva hit the polystyrene, it occurred to me that this practice should be considered a capital offence, preferably involving hanging, drawing and quartering – and thumbscrews.

I groaned.

My spitting fellow passenger was also very, very gay. His voice was the high-pitched, effeminate giggle of caricature. Either that, or he had attended an infant school where Liberace was on the teaching staff. I groaned again – a deep, masculine groan this time.

There was a pause, and the polystyrene spittoon received momentary relief. He spoke, apparently to me. We had not been introduced.

'First time in Denver?'

My mind raced with twenty replies, which included a lengthy statement about the fact that I have never found the male physique to be remotely attractive, that I love my wife, that I do not have a homophobic bone in my body, would never dream of dancing to 'YMCA', no, I'd been to

Denver before, and I'd never enjoyed Boy George's music that much.

'No, I've been to Denver before', I smiled – not too warmly. 'But I often fly into Colorado Springs via Denver.'

He spat again, forcefully this time. I had apparently said something very wrong. His nostrils flared and his eyes blazed. He explained that he hated Colorado Springs, because it was full of right-wing Christian conservatives, who were sworn, vocal enemies of his lifestyle. I looked frantically with one eye for an emergency exit. This man was totally unaware that he was sitting right next to a Christian, and a leader at that. This could get tricky.

I listened with gathering alarm as he told me how he had been 'de-baptised': a private ritual of his, designed to ceremonially renounce any allegiance to God and church. Catholicism, he continued, had been shoved down his neck from birth. And then came the question I was dreading.

'So. What do you do for a living?'

I coughed nervously and considered lying, but couldn't think of an occupation.

'I'm … a minister. Of the Christian kind.'

A long pause from him. Narrowing eyes. Pursed lips. At last he spoke.

'Minister, eh? You would probably line up with the right-wing conservative crowd.'

Again, my brain raced and I mentally bumped into potential sermonettes about Jesus loving sinners and hating sin, texts from the book of Romans, warning comments about AIDS and death and hell. I honestly couldn't think of what to say.

And so I just quietly explained why I followed Jesus. I said that Jesus had some radical things to say to all of us about sexuality – and not just homosexuality. But most of all, I apologised. I wanted this man to know that I felt shame about television evangelists who rant and rave and pick on certain types of sinners. I apologised because I felt that, too often, the church railed against the gay community rather than reaching out to them. I said sorry.

His eyes widened, and I thought that they were going to fill with tears. But he smiled a great warm smile, and put his hands together, prayer like.

'Jeff, I thank you for your words: I am humbled by them. And please know that I can see that Jesus Christ is at the centre of your being. Once again, I thank you.'

And then, remarkably, our friendship began. He scribbled his address down, and asked if Kay and I would join him for dinner in Denver. And three days later, he came to our hotel, and delivered complimentary tickets for our whole family for the Colorado Rockies' baseball game. Suspicion and enmity were sent packing by a simple expression of heartfelt regret. And in a few days, Kay and I will be in Denver for a dinner appointment. And it all started with … sorry.

ENOUGH SAID

The conference had been going rather well – my address on the opening evening had been well received. There was a spring in my step as I skipped down the hotel stairs, two at a time, heading towards the crowded lobby. Just time for a coffee before the first session of the day. Suddenly, a voice rang out from the landing above. Two ladies, delegates from the conference, had spotted me and decided to brighten my morning with a word of encouragement, which is always welcome. Their choice of words, however, caused quite a stir in the lobby.

'Jeff … heeeellooo … wait!'

I paused on the last stair, and looked up. They leaned over the stairwell, faces beaming, eyes bright with kindness.

'Jeff … both of us just wanted to say … thanks SO MUCH for last night …'

The teeming lobby instantly joined me in my pause, and looked at my reddening face with interest.

'You were ABSOLUTELY FANTASTIC last night …'

The lobby wrestled with moral outrage and veiled admiration.

'Yes, we both agree – we haven't laughed so much in years.'

I attempted a response of thanks but due to acute embarrassment, a high-pitched sound, like that of a chicken being strangled, emerged from my throat. Head down, I rushed out of the crowded lobby, avoiding the eyes of the other guests, some of whom clearly wanted me executed as a moral reprobate, and others who wanted to slap me heartily on the back and ask my secret. Of course, at one level, the exchange was rather refreshing in its naivety and simple purity, uncluttered by innuendo. I don't miss all that tiresome 'nudge nudge, wink wink' chatter from my pre-Christian days. But the other side of the story is that these delightful ladies, in their hurry to be kind, hadn't paused to consider their words – and their effect on the crowd in the lobby.

Something similar happened a few weeks ago at a major event that happens in the Spring when they're bringing the Harvest in. A lovely older lady rushed up to me after a seminar.

'I enjoyed that seminar, Jeff. Will you be speaking tonight?'

I replied in the negative. No, Steve Chalke would be speaking that evening.

'Oooooh, even better!' replied my erstwhile fan.

And as 'even better' emerged from her lips, her eyes screamed with alarm, as if she knew that her choice of words weren't the best: as if she was reaching frantically to catch them before they came tumbling out of her mouth … aaahh, too late.

I can't tell you how many times I wished that I had paused, just for one tiny second, before blurting out my thoughts. 'Slow to speak' is the biblical description of the Christian who engages the brain before releasing the mouth. A few seconds of deliberation and thought can save hours of recrimination and regret.

I conclude, therefore, with a formal apology to the lady that I met while on a hospital visit. She was visiting the same person as I, and smiled as I introduced myself. 'You must be the patient's mother,' I declared confidently, shaking her hand. The warm smile vanished, to be replaced by an icy glare big enough to sink the Titanic. 'No … I am her sister.'

Enough said.

THE ANONYMOUS LETTER

The anonymous letter is a frequently used communication technique, believe it or not, in some churches. Disgruntled and offended parishioners express their irritations to pastors and leaders by dispatching an unsigned epistle. The lack of signature and, therefore, the hidden identity of the writer, gives them the 'Dutch courage' needed to put the most toxic poison on paper. Scurrilous accusations, inferences and innuendoes jostle with each other in the grubby scrawl. The net effect on the recipient is devastating: it's like being hit by a relational exocet that comes screaming in from the dark, demolishing in a few seconds your confidence, your sense of calling, and hope.

Sadly, it's not a new idea. The famous evangelist D L Moody received such a poisonous pen letter while actually preaching a sermon. Someone out there in the congregation was apparently feeling highly uncomfortable, and so, hastily scratched out a note, and passed it back to an usher, who calmly walked up to the pulpit. The folded note had Mr Moody's name written on it, reasoned the hapless usher, so Mr Moody should receive the note, immediately. Moody took the note, unfolded it carefully, and read its brief content.

One word was written on the page: 'Fool'.

Moody sighed, re-folded the note, and made an announcement. 'I've just been sent a most unusual letter from one of you in the congregation', he said to a fairly shocked crowd.

'Now this is most interesting. I'm often sent letters where people write the body of the letter, but just omit their name. On this occasion, in writing the single word 'fool' the person concerned has omitted to write the letter itself, and has only signed their name'. He then proceeded with his sermon.

I saw the power of the anonymous letter while Kay and I were working on the staff of a church in Oregon. Having been a well-received part of the team for some eighteen months, we had felt that it was time to move on into a wider ministry of itinerant Bible teaching. An announcement was made to the church, advising them of our resignation and imminent departure. 'The letter' was sent to the senior minister and all of the deacons, but of course, Kay and I were not sent a copy by the anonymous writer. The letter alleged that the senior minister was jealous of the warm welcome that Kay and I had been shown, was nervous that we were popular, and so had acted to force us to leave. We were, the letter declared with the authority of one that knew, being driven out of town. The senior minister felt a high level of anxiety at this scandalous, and totally untrue, suggestion. I asked him to allow me to deal with the problem in my own way.

It was our final Sunday in the church, my leaving service, and I was preaching my last sermon. The place was packed. Time for some redemptive fun.

'Before I conclude, I want to let you know that the senior minister and the deacons of this church have each been sent a copy of a letter, a letter without signature, which accuses them of treating Kay and me badly, and suggesting that we are, and I quote, 'being driven out of town'.

I paused. Tension crackled in the air. I look round at John, the senior minister, who shifted from side to side on his seat on the platform. I continued.

'I have decided to tell you the unedited truth about the senior minister of this church and the deacons too. Hey, it's my last Sunday here, and I have nothing to lose – I currently have the microphone in hand – so why don't I just go ahead and spill the beans, as it were, on these people …'

The level of tension rose even higher. I decided to milk the moment. I walked back away from the pulpit and stood beside John. Placing my hand on his shoulder, I said, 'Let me just tell you the unbridled truth about this man. Again, what have I got to lose now? Let's go for broke.'

John looked up at me with pleading eyes, sweat breaking out now on his forehead. I had to wrap this up, if only to put poor John out of his misery.

'This man has done nothing – and I say again, nothing – but bless, shower kindness, encouragement, and help upon me, my family, and my ministry. He and the deacons of this church have done absolutely everything in their power to help resource and release me. I owe them a great debt. And so, to whomever it was that wrote the anonymous letter suggesting some kind of ridiculous conspiracy, I would like to say two things. First, check your facts, because you couldn't be more wrong. And second, next time you sit down to put pen to paper, have the moral courage to sign your name at the bottom of the letter. An unsigned letter is not worthy of the time needed to read it. It is a work of cowardice. Whoever wrote it, please hear me say this loud and clear: you need to repent.'

I sat down, and the congregation rose to their feet in what was, not a standing ovation for me, but a message of love and endorsement for John and the team of deacons that served with him. I looked at the crowd whooping, yelling, and waving their Bibles, and realised that someone, somewhere out there in the crowd, was the author of the anonymous letter.

Operation World

Patrick Johnstone

Packed with inspiring fuel for prayer about every country and major people group on the globe, Operation World is essential reading for anyone who wants to make a difference to our world.

Following on from the phenomenal success of previous editions, Operation World is now available in a new, fully revised 21st-century edition containing over 80 per cent new material. For the first time in the history of Operation World, answers to prayers have been detailed within the text for encouragement.

Operation World will help you turn world news into spiritual dynamite!

Paternoster Lifestyle
ISBN: 1-8507.8357-8

Price: £14.99

£9.99 with voucher

First published in 2001 by Paternoster Lifestyle

Paternoster Lifestyle is an imprint of Paternoster Publishing
PO Box 300, Kingstown Broadway, Carlisle, Cumbria, CA3 0QS

Afghanistan

Islamic Emirate of afghanistan

FEBRUARY 7 – 8
ASIA

GEOGRAPHY

Area 652,225 sq.km. Dry and mountainous, but with fertile valleys. This strategic land has been fought over by rival foreign empires for nearly three thousand years.

Population		Ann.Gr.	Density
2000	22,720,000	+2.93%	35 per sq. km.
2010	32,902,000	+2.58%	50 per sq. km.
2025	44,934,000	+1.95%	69 per sq. km.

No census or careful ethnic survey has ever been made. Figures are all estimates. Afghan refugees in 2000 numbered 1.4 million in Iran, 2.2 to 3 million in Pakistan and smaller numbers across the world after peaking in the 1990s at 6.5 million.

Capital Kabul 2,700,000. The civil war extensively damaged the capital. Other cities: Kandahar 420,000; Mazar-e-Sharif 270,000. **Urbanites** 22%.

PEOPLES

70 peoples.

Indo-Iranian 86.8%. Largest: Pashtun (Pathan) 9.7mill.; Tajik 4m; Hazara/Aimaq (of Turkic origin) 1.8m; Other Persian-speaking 770,000; Baluch 260,000; Nuristani peoples(11) 250,000.

Turkic-speaking 10.7%. 10 peoples. Uzbek 1.8m; Turkmen 520,000.

Other 2.5%. Brahui 240,000; Pashai 160,000.

Literacy 10-31% (much lower for women).

Official languages Pashto (used by 50% of population), Dari (Afghan Persian, 35%). **All languages** 50.

Languages with Scriptures 2NT 3por.

ECONOMY

Shattered by 22 years of war. The coun-tryside was bombed and mined; half the housing, most of the complex irrigation systems and a high proportion of the livestock were destroyed. The most lucrative agricultural crop is now opium (Afghanistan is the world's largest producer) which has paid for weapons for the warring factions. Recovery has been slowed by the radical extremes of the

Taliban government and widespread environmental and structural damage inflicted on this tragic land. **HDI** n.a. **Public debt** 95% of GNP. Income/person $250 (0.8% of USA).

POLITICS

The monarchy was overthrown in 1973. Republican government ended in a Marxist coup in 1978. Then followed an invasion by the USSR. Ten years of war ensued culminating in the humiliating withdrawal of the Soviet forces in 1988-89. Civil war between ethnic and religious factions has continued ever since with enormous damage and casualties. The extreme Islamist (mainly) Pashtun Taliban gained control of over 90% of the country by 2001. UN sanctions in 2001 further isolated the country.

RELIGION

The Taliban take-over of the country has imposed the strictest interpretation of Islam in the world today. The results have been devastating for the economy and for the lot of women in society. All Afghans must comply with the strict codes imposed on dress, beards, education and

Religions	Population %	Adherents	Ann.Gr.
Muslim	97.89	22,241,015	+2.9
Parsee	1.50	340,806	+2.9
Hindu	0.35	79,521	+0.2
Traditional ethnic	0.10	22,720	+2.9
Baha'i	0.10	22,720	n.a.
Christian	0.02	3,000	n.a.
Sikh	0.02	4,544	+2.9
non-Religious	0.01	2,272	+2.9

observance of *shari'a* law. What little religious freedom existed has been terminated.

Non-Muslim figures may be now much lower than these stated. No Christian churches are permitted. The number of Afghan Christians is estimated to be 1,000 to 3,000. Some Christian expatriate workers have been permitted to serve in relief and social uplift programmes.

Challenges for Prayer

1 **The largely Pashtun Taliban** swept to power with Pakistani military support, U.S. arms and Saudi money. Traditional and rural in outlook and using Islam to legitimate their authority, they have imposed a measure of stability after 22 years of war. A narrow interpretation of *shari'a* law has outlawed playing games, use of cassette tapes, videos and TV (and much more) and has tyrannized the Shi'a Muslims, women and anyone deviating from the Taliban's interpretation of the law. In 2001 the death penalty was imposed for any-one converting from Islam or attempting to convert anyone from Islam. Pray that the unprecedented openness to the gospel created by these sufferings may ultimately lead to a great harvest.

2 **Two decades of unremitting war** have brought most of the population to ruin and destitution. An estimated 1 million lost their lives, 2 million were maimed and 4 million children orphaned. The result is ecological disaster, a shattered infrastructure, over 12 million uncleared anti-personnel mines and the capital in ruins. Pray for peace, recon-struction, an awakening to moderation and tolerance and a realization that Marxism and Islam cannot provide the solutions to heal their land.

3 **Afghanistan has become an open, festering wound that is poisoning the world**. Though most Taliban are nationalists, violent pan-Islamists have also joined the movement with the aim of exporting Islamist revolution to surrounding lands. The opium harvest is now the world's largest with production the equivalent of $35 billion a year. Pray for a just, fair and honourable government to be raised up for this tragic land.

4 **Afghanistan is one of the least reached countries in the world**. There are 48,000 mosques but not a single church building. Pray for the 70 unreached peoples of this land, especially:

a) *Pashtun. Approx*imately half the Afghan population, and politically dominant, the Pashtuns on both sides of the Afghanistan-Pakistan border comprise what has been called the largest Muslim tribal society in the world — approximately 27 million people in over 30 major sub-tribes. There are few Christians among them, though urban, educated Pashtuns in exile have shown responsiveness. Pray that multitudes might be released from the strongholds of Islam, fear, prejudice and pride in pashtunwali (their tribal code of honour).

b) *Uzbek and Turkmen* of the north have shown some responsiveness as refugees in other lands. Their whole way of life is under threat from the Taliban regime.

c) *Tajik* in the north-east. They are among the last people to resist the Taliban. Pray for their spiritual freedom.

d) *The Hazara* , Shi'a Muslims of Mongol descent, have been severely persecuted and even massacred by the Sunni Taliban. More responsive to the gospel in recent years.

e) *The Kuchi nomads* in central and western regions who numbered 2.5m before the war destroyed their life-style. Most are Pashto- or Persian-speaking. Many fled to Pakistan.

f) *The Aimaq* of the west and the *Baluch* and *Brahui* of the south.

g) *The Nuristani tribes* in the mountains north and east of Kabul. They speak a number of mutually unintelligible languages. The major peoples are the Waigeli 40,000; Kati 100,000; Ashkun 10,000. They were forcibly converted to Islam a century ago. Some parts of Nuristan were much influenced in the 1990s by Wahhabism, a strict Islamic sect, very hostile to anything Christian.

h) *The Sikh, Hindu and Parsee minorities* who are mainly traders.

5 **Though there is no visible church** in Afghanistan, the number of Afghan believers is increasing in urban and some remote rural areas. Because of fear and suspicion, many believers find it difficult to meet in groups. Some find help and encouragement through Christian radio programmes in the main languages of Afghanistan. The Taliban religious police are active in seeking out 'converts' who are considered apostates. Pray for their protection, consistency of faith and clarity of witness whenever opportunity arises. Pray also that the small fellowships (many are family groups) of Afghan Christians that have come into being in South Asia, Europe and North America may become bold witnesses for Christ.

6 **Women in the cities** have been severely repressed by the Taliban regime. They have been banished from public life, forbidden employment, restricted to the home,

denied education (girls) and health services and suffer at the hands of men, with no recourse to any justice. One in four women are widows, and many are destitute. Depression and suicide are commonplace. Pray for basic human rights to be restored to women.

7 **Christian aid ministries**. Since 1966 a number of Christian relief and development agencies have ministered to the blind, maimed, sick, deprived, illiterate and needy in the name and Spirit of the Lord Jesus. Pray for courage in the face of severe restrictions or constant harassment and that their lives might commend the gospel. Pray that professionals may respond to the many needs of these Christian NGOs.

8 **The need for the Scriptures**. The whole Bible is available in Iranian Persian, but differences between this and Afghan Persian makes it difficult for many to read. A translation of the Bible was made in the 19th Century but this is unavailable and its language archaic. The NT in Dari (Afghan Persian) and in a Pakistani dialect of Pashto have been well received. Translations into major dialects of Afghan Pashto are still needed. The OT is slowly progressing in Dari and Pashto; pray for their speedy completion. Translations do not exist in any indigenous minority language. Pray that these might come to fruition. Pray also for the entry and distribution of God's word in this closed land, which the Taliban is seeking to prevent.

9 **The Media**. Pray that all appropriate methods of witness may be used effectively.
a) *GRN* (LRI) has made audio recordings in 38 languages and dialects but means for effective distribution and use are, humanly-speaking, virtually non-existent in Afghanistan.

b) ***Christian radio***. This is the most strategic way to
   proclaim the good news at the present time and there
   has been a significant response. **FEBA**, with **IBRA** as
   partners, broadcast in Persian (4.5 hrs/wk), Dari (5),
   Pashto (3.25), Uzbek (1.75) and also Baluch and
   Turkmen. Pray for the provision of and support for
   more Dari- and Pashto-speaking Christians to prepare
   programmes and answer mail. Pray also for programming to commence in other Afghan languages.

c) ***The JESUS film*** is available in Brahui, Dari, Pashto,
   Tajik, Turkmen and Uzbek, but its use inside Afghanistan is difficult at the present time.

d) ***Literature***. Discipleship and other training materials
   are being developed in the major languages of Afghanistan, in addition to many other types of evangelistic
   materials. Though forbidden for distribution or
   possession inside Afghanistan, this has been very effective in reaching Afghans in exile. Pray for those
   involved in producing, distributing and studying these
   materials.

UNITED KINGDOM — GENERAL

Answers to Prayer

1 **The cease-fire in the Northern Ireland 'Troubles'** has largely been maintained since 1998.

2 **Evangelical Christians are basically maintaining numbers**, despite considerable church decline, and are becoming more prominent in mainline denominations. Some newer movements and innovative post-modern culture churches are growing.

3 **Some ethnic minorities** have been more receptive with considerable growth in African-initiated churches, multi-ethnic churches and also over 6,000 'Travellers' (Roma/Gypsy) coming to Christ in the past few years (Gypsy Evangelical Movement).

Challenges for Prayer

1 **Britain needs to regain a sense of purpose and direction for the 21st Century**. The nation is torn between its European geography and its Atlanticist culture. Pray that political leadership may have the moral integrity

and courage to give the correct lead. Membership of the EU and differing views on the degree of federalism desirable and its impact on national life is a matter for intense public concern and debate.

2 **A sense that all is not well pervades the country.** The 'freedoms' of the 1960s led to social disaster and hastened spiritual decline. Many are discouraged about the future and cynical about the seeming impotence of politicians to deal with the malaise. The gay rights movement, though representing a small minority, has seized the initiative in many areas of public life and in government legislation. Spiritual need is highlighted by increasing violence in the cities, the high divorce, suicide and illegitimacy rates, and drug abuse. Paralleling this is the growing number of younger people who have no contact with or knowledge of Christianity. Without a radical change, disaster looms. Pray for national repentance and restoration to the spiritual vigour that once made Britain's Christians a blessing to the world.

3 **A national awakening is needed.** There has been one every century in the last 800 years — the last was in 1859-69. The Judeo-Christian heritage has been so eroded by post-modernist worldviews that public opinion is no longer Christian. Christians have been marginalized in the media, public life, government legislation and school curricula. Religious pluralization has sapped the confidence of many Christians to testify boldly and even believe that Jesus is the only way to the Father. The steep decline in numbers of the Methodists, Anglicans, United Reformed, Brethren and other denominations continues and the Baptists and newer (house) churches have plateaued. Pray that Christians might become passionate for God's honour, burdened to

pray for revival and be freed from a deadening negativism and materialism that pervades the life of the churches.

4 **Tolerance is the 'in' word.** The influx of non-Christian religions has affected the worldview of the population. The spokesmen for Islam, Buddhism, Hinduism, etc., push for legislation that will favour their religions, and demand freedoms they would never grant Christians in their lands of origin. Astrology, the occult, reincarnation, old world paganism (Druid/Wicca) and even Satanism have become popular, with a massive increase in literature promoting their ends. The mission field has come to the UK — and many non-Western Christians perceive the UK itself as a mission field. Pray that UK Christians may recover a confidence in the 'intolerant' gospel and a passion for sharing it with the majority who have little concept of its content.

5 **The future of the Church of England is crucial for the country** and is the 'mother' Church for the world's 80 million Anglicans. This composite body is an umbrella under which Anglo-Catholics, liberals and Evangelicals co-exist and where, tragically, equivocation on homosexuality and the basic tenets of the Christian faith are condoned. Fragmentation of the Church over such issues as ordination of women, ecumenism and dis-establishment is possible. Yet Evangelicalism is a growing force and gaining centre stage: 27% of bishops, 53% of clergy, 60% of ordinands and 40% of church-goers espouse its cause. The 1998 Lambeth Conference of the Anglican Communion was a resounding setback for liberalism as the non-Western majority strongly affirmed biblical values. The charismatic movement has also contributed to an extensive renewal movement in the Church. Pray that

Church leadership might regain a prophetic role and speak with clear biblical authority to a nation that is morally and spiritually adrift.

6 **There are signs of hope** — water these tender plants with prayer:

a) *Traumatic social change* and the devastating consequences of violence, family break-down and fear for the future have brought a new openness to consider spiritual solutions.

b) *Renewal movements.* Many pastors and congregations experienced charismatic renewal between the 1960s-'80s. This also gave rise to a new family of churches. The house church movement, or Newer Churches, grew fast and have become a significant spiritual force in the nation, deeply affecting church structures and fellowship patterns, and have enlivened worship across the denominational spectrum. Their growth slowed in the 1990s. Nation-wide, these changes have been stimulated by major trans-denominational gatherings such as Greenbelt and Spring Harvest.

c) *New younger generation movements* are emerging with radically new approaches — Internet café gatherings, WEB prayer and culturally appropriate worship styles, such as Tribal Generation, flowing from the Church of England, and also others spontaneously springing up in different parts of the country.

d) *The Alpha Course phenomenon* has spread across the country to nearly every denomination and across the world as one of the most successful outreach programmes run by churches in the UK today. These user-friendly   introductory   courses   explain

Christianity in a relaxed and informal environment. About 6,400 congregations were using the Alpha courses in 1998 with over 650,000 individuals having completed one.

e) *Christian leaders* from across the denominational spectrum are meeting regularly for prayer together in many cities and towns. This is leading to cooperative efforts in ministry.

7 **Evangelical Christianity** has grown slowly in percentage of the population, of church-goers and as a proportion of active membership in mainline denominations, but there are definite challenges:

a) *To maintain and increase unity* in fellowship and vision. **The Evangelical Alliance** has done much to encourage this and give credibility to Evangelicals in national life. The EA represents 1.3 million Evangelicals, 30 denominations and 800 agencies.

b) *A widespread loss of confidence* and certainty about models for church life and out-reach. There were a number of initiatives in the 1990s which fizzled out or did not halt the overall malaise and decline.

c) *A common cynicism about the future* and the state of the Kingdom of God in the world which cripples enthusiasm for missions locally or overseas. Pray for restoration of vision and faith in God's ability to change Britain once more.

8 **Christian leadership** is under intense pressure — church members are more demanding, less committed, giving less and often more interested in self-fulfilment than sacrificial service. There is a lack of effective Bible teachers and expositors. Pray for effective discipling and training of a new generation of leaders in

both congregational and more formal theological
training. There were 59 residential denominational
colleges and 25 interdenominational colleges with a
total of 7,150 students in 1999. Pray that these may not
only impart a theological education, but also spirituality
and world vision.

9 Young people are more spiritually open, but increasingly come from dysfunctional families, a history of
drug abuse and promiscuous lifestyles. They need intense,
loving help to become effective disciples. Pray for:

a) *Religious education teachers* in schools. RE is a core
   subject by law but is often ignored, resisted or even
   opposed by school authorities and students. Pray for
   Christians involved in this ministry and for meaningful ways of making the message of the gospel
   come alive.

b) *Commitment* to Jesus and His will, to the discipline of
   Bible study and to the church. Few have come from a
   background of church life.

c) *Effective discipling of children*. Sunday School is a
   fading institution and viable alternative models are
   lacking.

d) *Youth movements.* Covenanters, Crusaders, SU and
   British YFC have long had significant impact. Newer
   movements such as Soul Survivor and Oasis are
   proving innovative and effective.

e) *Missions vision* — few young people have much
   exposure to a vision for the world. Theministries of
   OM, World Horizons, YWAM and Worldwide
   Message Tribe are seeking to redress this with
   short-term training and exposure.

10 **Students** are exposed to great pressures in the secular education system. A largely godless and materialistic younger generation is being formed by it. Relatively few secondary schools have a live, outgoing witness from staff or student groups. Pray for:

a) *The SU and Christian Union groups* in schools — for their growth and multiplication, and for Christian teachers to be used of God to help launch such groups.

b) *The Campus Christian groups* among the 900,000 full-time students in colleges and universities. Their growth and diversity is encouraging, the main ones being Agapé (**CCCI**), **Navigators**, Fusion and UCCF(**IFES**). The oldest and most widespread is the work of UCCF with Christian Unions in nearly 600 colleges and universities, yet a further 300 have no permanent group. Pray for mature, stable leadership, effective support and advice from the 45 travelling secretaries, and establishment of a viable witness in every college. The student population is one of the more receptive segments of society.

c) *Overseas students.* About 400,000 overseas students are granted visas every year — 80,000 to do university degrees. Outreach to them is varied but too limited, and many return home without ever hearing the gospel. UCCF(**IFES**), International Student Christian Services with 40 staff in 18 cities, In Contact Ministries, and others have ministry to them.

11 **Britain's contribution to world evangelization** in the last 200 years is unique. Interest has waned and many congregations have never even sent out their own missionary. In 2000 there was only one Protestant missionary overseas for every 6 churches. There

is a widespread conviction that either the job has been done or that efforts should be concentrated on Britain's need. Pray for:

a) *A renewed commitment* by local congregations to world evangelization, to pray out their members to the areas of greatest need, and to care adequately for those who go.

b) *An increase in recruitment* for missions; pray that the growth in short-term involvement may lead to increased long-term recruitment and support.

c) *The coordinating role of Global Connections* (EMA) in promoting vision and cooperation among mission agencies and in local churches for world evangelization.

12 **The growing non–Anglo-Saxon minority** has become a significant part of UK urban life in the past 50 years. Many cities have large minority communities and in some they have become the majority. Some communities such as the Afro-Caribbean and Chinese have a higher proportion of active Christians than the indigenous population. Others come from countries where the gospel is little known and entry of missionaries impeded. Cultural distance, racial discrimination and even open hostility have antagonized many against 'Christianity'. Pray for:

a) *Local congregations* in multi-ethnic areas to open their doors, homes and hearts to this mission field on their doorstep, and to find effective ways of making friendships, meeting needs and winning some for the Lord.

b) *Specialist cross-cultural workers* to be called both for training churches and ministering to specific ethnic groups. Unique ministries already involved: **South**

Asian Concern, **OM** (Turning Point), **YWAM**, **In Contact Ministries**, and also missionaries linked with **Interserve**, **ECM**, **MECO**, **BCMS Crosslinks**, **WEC**, **IMI**, **IT**, **RSTI** as well as non-Western mission agencies.

c) *Better coordination of effort and research of the need.* **South Asia Concern** has completed a detailed survey of the 1.5 million South Asians. Many ethnic minority communities are completely unreached due to lack of information to mobilize a ministry to reach them.

d) *Effective use of literature and other media.* Some **CLC** bookstores stock minority language literature. **WEC**'s 'SOON' broadsheet ministry in English, Panjabi, French, Hindi, Swahili, Urdu and Arabic reaches many. In Contact Ministries specializes in literature on Islamics and in ethnic minority languages.

13 **Specific ethnic minority groups** that need intercession:

a) *Caribbean and African peoples.* There are over 200 denominations; 20% of the population is church-going. In the past, these churches have been somewhat isolated from the mainstream of evangelical Christianity. The African Caribbean Evangelical Alliance (ACEA) is committed to creating an equitable partnership through their programmes of networking and community building. Pray that ACEA may be able to continue giving a sense of unity to these churches and help them to combat the growing social and economic problems faced by the black community in general.

b) *South Asians.* An increasing number of people are coming to Christ from the Hindu and Sikh communities, but few from among Muslims; about 4% of all South Asians are Christian. The greatest need is among the Panjabi, Kashmiri, Bangladeshi and Pathan communities.

c) *Middle Eastern peoples.* Outreach is largely localized and sporadic. Many wealthy **Arabs** come to the UK as tourists, businessmen and students; some have come to faith. There are several Christian fellowships for Arabs and a few for the **Turks, Kurds** and **Iranians**. There is also a Bible Training School (**ELAM Ministries** for preparing Iranians for ministry. The **Yemenis** and 50,000 **Moroccans** are unreached.

d) *Muslims* now officially number over 1.2 million, but the actual number is probably much higher. About ½ from Pakistan, ¼ from the Middle East and a further ¼ from India and Bangladesh. Large-scale illegal immigration, and an increasingly strident radical Islam of a minority that seeks to alter British society in favour of Islam, have helped to alienate Muslims from the indigenous majority. Muslims see the conversion of England to Islam as a key strategy for winning Europe. London has become a hub for extreme, militant Islamist organizations. Pray for a breakdown of cultural and social barriers on both sides and for opportunities to be created for sharing the gospel.

e) *Chinese.* They have mainly come from Hong Kong and Vietnam, but increasingly from Mainland China as illegal immigrants and students. The Chinese Overseas Christian Mission (**COCM**) has a successful church planting and student ministry. There are around 70 Chinese churches and about 7% of Chinese are Christian.

f) *The Jewish community.* This is slowly declining through assimilation (80% have no religious commitment to Judaism) and marriage. Many are disillusioned by the rigid legalism and internal squabbling of communal leaders. Many of the believers integrate into Gentile churches, though there are also eight fellowships of Messianic Jews and possibly about 2,000 believers altogether. Pray for the ministry of CMJ, **MT**, **CWI** and **Jews for Jesus**. There is increasing opposition to such ministry both from Jewish anti-missionary groups and from liberal Christian circles.

14 **Christian media ministries:**

a) *Christian literature and Bibles.* Few nations have such an extensive range of Christian literature, Bible versions and the facilities to acquire them. **The Gideons International** distributed 20 million NTs and Bibles in their first 40 years of ministry. In 2000 there were 506 Christian bookstores carrying an average of 3,600 titles! There are over 100 Christian publishers publishing 4,400 new titles annually. **The Bible Societies** not only have a ministry of Bible translation, publication and distribution in Britain and around the world, but also a wide range of catalytic ministries to stimulate Christian growth. **BookAid** has a remarkable ministry of exporting one million surplus and second-hand Christian books annually to poorer countries. Pray for these ministries and for Christians to become more avid readers.

b) *Christian broadcasting.* The 1990 Broadcasting Act opened unprecedented opportunities for Christians to own radio stations, satellite and cable TV stations. Pray for wisdom and balance in the face of opportunities. Many Christians are active in secular broad-casting as well as religious programming on national radio and television — over 6 million view Songs of Praise every week. Pray for positive impact. All efforts at ending the BBC's monopoly on (increasingly multi-faith) national, terrestrial religious broad-casting have failed — pray for change.

Live Like a Jesus Freak

dc Talk

Being a Jesus Freak is all about following Jesus. He never promised it would be easy. Quite the opposite! Look at his words: 'If anyone would come after me, he must deny himself and take up his cross and follow me. For whoever wants to save his life will lose it, but whoever loses his life for me will find it' (Matthew 16:24–25).

Through an eclectic mix of challenging essays, discussion-generating questions and testimonies of people changed by the original Jesus Freaks book, this book will help you to live like a Jesus freak too!

Eagle Publishing
ISBN: 0-8634-7501-9

Price: £7.99

£5.99 with voucher

Published in 2001 by Eagle Publishing
6-7 Leapale Road, Guildford, Surrey, GU1 4JX

Introduction

Welcome to the Freak Zone — the Jesus Freak Zone. If you're reading this book, you must want to live a radical life for Jesus. Why else would you bother to open these pages? In the following ten chapters you'll discover the why and how behind what it means to be a Jesus Freak. You'll learn why standing out from the crowd is a good thing. Most of all, you'll catch a glimpse of the fact that as a Jesus Freak you're in good company — the very best, in fact.

> Do you see what this means — all these pioneers who blazed the way, all these veterans cheering us on? It means we'd better get on with it. Strip down, start running — and never quit! No extra spiritual fat, no parasitic sins. Keep your eyes on Jesus, who both began and finished this race we're in. Study how he did it. Because he never lost sight of where he was headed — that exhilarating finish in and with God — he could put up with anything along the way: cross, shame, whatever. And now he's there, in the place of honor, right alongside God.
>
> — HEBREWS 12:1–2, THE MESSAGE

One word of warning: This book is not a prescription for a safe, comfortable life. Nor is it a syllabus for Spirituality

101. And it's definitely not a script for a "junior" version of your parents' religion (you knew that anyway, right?). When Jesus crashed onto the human scene 2,000 years ago, He turned the world upside down. The same Man who turned over the moneychangers' tables – and conventional ideas of how to reach God – is still in the business of wreaking Godly havoc on people's lives. Are you ready to take the plunge?

Before you became a Jesus Freak, you might have been known as bold and wild, a fearless person with a "bring it on!" attitude. Now you want to channel that energy into a committed relationship with God, but you're not sure how to go about it. Or maybe you were the quiet, shy type, always feeling as if you were on the outside looking in. Now that Jesus rules your life, you're ready to move off the fringes and into the fray – into the Freak Zone.

Jesus never promised that being His follower would be easy. Quite the opposite, in fact. Look at His words:

> If anyone would come after me, he must deny himself and take up his cross and follow me. For whoever wants to save his life will lose it, but whoever loses his life for me will find it.
> – MATTHEW 16:24–25

Toward the end of His life on earth, Jesus set out on the road to Jerusalem with His disciples. As they journeyed through dusty villages on the way to the Holy City, they bumped into would-be Jesus Freaks along the way.

One man told Jesus he would follow Him anywhere – but first he needed to bury his father. Jesus' reply seems harsh when we read it today, but He was deliberately making a point: "Let the dead bury their own dead, but you go and proclaim the kingdom of God."

Still another said, "I will follow You, Lord, but first let me go back and say good-bye to my family." Using a cultural image the man would understand, Jesus told him that no one who puts his hand to the plow and looks back is fit to serve God. In other words, you're either in this or you're not — no turning back.

What about you? Is something holding you back from all-out commitment Christ' Before you wade into the pages of this book, deep into your soul — the real you. Are you ready to forsake all and follow Him? Are you ready to ...

Live Like a Jesus Freak?

"While we may not be called to martyr our lives, we must martyr our way of life. We must put our selfish ways to death and march to a different beat. Then the world will see Jesus."

      — Michael Tait of dc Talk[1]

---

[1] From *Jesus Freaks* by dc Talk and the Voice of the Martyrs (Eagle Publishing: Guildford Uk 2000).

Chapter One

Believe Like a Jesus Freak

In 1990, the world of pop culture learned a startling truth:
The two young men who comprised pop sensation Milli
Vanilli never sang a note of their mega-selling album, *Girl
You Know It's True*. Instead, they were nothing more than
"techno-puppets," as one writer put it, lip-synching songs
for a studio-manufactured sound that sold 10 million cop-
ies. Forced to go public with the truth, the two men told
the press a bizarre rags-to-riches story that sounded like an
MTV version of *Oliver Twist*. The public scorned Rob
Pilatus and Fabrice Morvan for the fakes they turned out
to be. And the National Academy of Recording Arts and
Sciences delivered the final blow, reclaiming the Best New
Artist Grammy it had awarded the duo.

Everybody despises a fake. If you wear a façade, sooner
or later the real you will show through. When it finally
does, you'd better be prepared to deal with the consequences! That's what happened to the religious leaders of
Jesus' day. They paraded around wearing holy-looking
robes. They made a show of their long-winded,
pious-sounding prayers. And they always bagged a
front-row seat at key events. After all, they were the big

cheeses, the spiritual elite of their day – and everybody knew it.

Jesus saw through the Pharisees' façade. He blasted them for their fake religiosity, comparing them to sheep in wolves' clothing and a pit of snakes. When it comes to religion, it seems that the twenty-first century is no different from the first century.

It takes courage to live a bold, passionate life for Christ in today's world.

While phoniness earns our disrespect and anger, truthfulness is respected, even when it's unpopular. As a Jesus Freak, you probably already know there will be times when you will stand out from the crowd because of your beliefs. Maybe the popular crowd laughs at you; perhaps your old friends avoid you. Jesus told us to expect that – it comes with the territory when we deny our old lifestyle and "take up our cross" to follow Him. Even though you may suffer ridicule, deep down those same people probably respect you.

The reality is that even popular culture admires courage. Courage in action is a common movie theme:

A young woman in a mental hospital stands up to the testing of the psych-ward bully, earning her grudging respect and even her friendship in the end. (Girl, Interrupted)

A famous author-turned-recluse befriends a young urban male, teaching him the finer points of writing. When his cherished anonymity is threatened, he chooses to go public to save his young friend's reputation. (Finding Forrester)

Two lifelong friends fight side by side in World War II. Although they both love the same woman, one friend takes a bullet for the other and gives up the possibility of a life with her. (Pearl Harbor)

It takes courage to live a bold, passionate life for Christ in today's world. In our gut, we all know nothing less will do. But you may be asking, "How can I consistently live what I believe?" It's a fair question. The temptation to cave in to the peer pressure around you is a daily battle, and the messages sent by the media aren't exactly growing tamer by the day. How can Jesus Freaks maintain their integrity? How can Jesus Freaks do more than give lip service to their faith? As an earlier generation used to say, how can Jesus Freaks "walk the talk"?

"What Will People Do When They Find Out It's True?"

It was the late 1930s. Hitler's war machine was ravaging one European country after another. Corrie ten Boom was a single Dutch woman who lived quietly above her father's watch shop. She was about to have her life shaken to the core. As the Gestapo moved in to the town of Haarlem the narrow creaking old house harbored not only Corrie's close-knit family but also a secret room – a hiding place for Jews hoping to escape the Nazi concentration camps.

Recalling the day in January 1937 when she, her sister, and her father celebrated the watch shop's 100th anniversary, Corrie wrote in her book *The Hiding Place*.

"How could we have guessed as we sat there ... that in place of memories we were about to be given adventure such as we had never dreamed of? Adventure and anguish, horror and heaven were just around the corner, and we did not know. Oh Father! Betsie! If I had known, would I have gone ahead? Could I have done the things I did?"

As the Nazis invaded Holland, the ten Boom family operated an "underground" operation that fed, clothed, and housed Jews – and often spirited them away to safety. When the Nazis discovered their scheme, Corrie and Betsie were shipped off to prison and eventually landed in Ravensbrück, one of the most notorious concentration camps.

With the help of a smuggled Bible, the sisters dispensed hope and the gospel to their fellow inmates, and gradually watched a divine pattern unfold. Before she died in Ravensbrück, Betsie told Corrie, "Your whole life has been a training ground for the work you are doing here in prison – and the work you will do afterward."

After her release from Ravensbrück, Corrie traveled the globe as a self-described "tramp for the Lord," sharing her story with thousands. One day, as she spoke at a church service in post-war Munich, she saw a face she recognized – a face that made her stomach clench with hatred. It was the guard who had stood watch over the shower room door at Ravensbrück. And now here he was making his way to the front, his eyes on her!

The man – who could not have recognized her – stopped in front of Corrie and thrust out his hand. "How grateful I am for your message, Fräulein. To think that, as you say, He has washed my sins away!"

Corrie froze. This was a test, and she knew it – was her faith real, or was she just paying lip service to God? Jesus had said, "Love your enemies ... pray for those which despitefully use you" (Matthew 5:44 kjv). Sending up a silent prayer for supernatural forgiveness, she extended her hand in return. As she did, "the most incredible thing happened," she writes. "From my shoulder along my arm and through my hand a current seemed to pass from me to him, while into my heart sprang a love for this stranger that almost overwhelmed me. And so I discovered that it is not on our forgiveness any more than on our goodness that the world's healing hinges, but on His. When He tells us to love our enemies, He gives, along with the command, the love itself."[2]

God fuels us with supernatural power to live and love the way Christ did when he walked the earth.

Do you have the courage to offer love when it may be thrown back in your face?

Are you willing to share your story – the story of how you became a Jesus Freak – even if it means people may laugh and walk away?

God fuels us with supernatural power to live and love the way Christ did when He walked the earth.

Strong Faith in the Dry Seasons

Loneliness. Depression. A "who-cares" attitude toward God. We all feel like this from time to time, but as Jesus Freaks we put pressure on ourselves – and others – to nip "downer" moods in the bud. *Jesus is still Lord, right?* we tell

---

[2] From *The Hiding Place* (reissue edition) by Corrie ten Boom (Bantam Books: NY, 1984).

ourselves, trying to prop up our emotions with a self-induced pep talk. The Bible, and history itself, abounds with stories of Jesus Freaks who faced their share of hard times. What was their secret to going the distance? How did they stay true to Christ in the long haul? Listen to the words of one famous Jesus Freak who experienced high "highs" and low "lows":

> Save me, God!
> I am about to drown.
> I am sinking deep in the mud,
> and my feet are slipping.
> I am about to be swept under by a mighty flood.
> I am worn out from crying,
> and my throat is dry.
> I have waited for you
> till my eyes are blurred.
>
> — PSALM 69:1–3 CEV

David wasn't timid about airing his troubles and frustrations with God – he did not try to hide what he was feeling. At the same time, he recognized that his strength and hope could only be found in the Lord. Two psalms later we hear him proclaiming:

> I will never give up hope
> or stop praising you.
> All day long I will tell
> the wonderful things you do
> to save your people.
> But you have done much more
> than I could possibly know …
> You made me suffer a lot,

but you will bring me
back from this deep pit
and give me new life.

– PSALM 71:14–15, 20 CEV

"Fits of depression come over most of us," the great nine-teenth-century preacher Charles Spurgeon once said to his students. "The strong are not always vigorous, the joyous are not always happy."

Spurgeon sure knew what he was talking about. Even though he is considered one of history's greatest preachers, he was prone to agonizing periods of depression. He suffered a horrible bout of discouragement when he was only twenty-two years old. Frustrated that his congregation had outgrown its building, Spurgeon booked a large concert hall in London. As he stood to speak on Sunday morning, he said, "We shall be gathered together tonight where an unprecedented mass of people will assemble, perhaps from idle curiosity, to hear God's Word; see what God can do, just when a cloud is falling on the head of him whom God has raised up to preach to you."

That night 12,000 people packed Surrey Hall; another 10,000 overflowed into the gardens. But someone started a hoax fire alarm, and hearing the cries of "Fire! Fire!" the crowd stampeded in panic, trampling seven people to death. Spurgeon collapsed from shock and was taken to a friend's house to recover. He remained in seclusion for weeks, begging God to reveal the why behind what had happened. Finally, while meditating on Scripture, his spirit and health were revived. Incredibly, that disaster was the catalyst for Charles Spurgeon's overnight fame as a preacher of the gospel.

The verse that triggered Spurgeon's restoration were these simple words from Philippians 2:10: *"… that at the name of Jesus every knee should bow, in heaven and on earth and under the earth."*

Like the love relationship between a man and a woman, our love for God will go through ups and downs. That's only natural. God made us who we are, and the Bible says He remembers that we are clay. He knows we sometimes have doubts and go through times of uncertainty. King David and Corrie ten Boom went through such times. But be courageous. Even if you can't see or feel God at a crucial moment, know that He has promised to never leave you. And He always keeps his promises.

How can you consistently live what you believe?
How can people know from your life that Jesus is real?

When your faith wavers or discouragement piles up on you, where do you turn?

What three things can you say or do the next time you enter a "dry season" in your life as a Jesus Freak?

(Hint: Check out Psalm 71 again.)

Jesus Freaks Around You Now

The Cigarette Sermons

Linh Dao, Vietnam, 1991
Four police officers suddenly burst into ten-year-old Linh Dao's home. They forced her father, an underground pastor in North Vietnam, to remain seated while the authorities ransacked the home, searching for Bibles.

"I remember when the police came," Linh Dao recalls. "They searched around the house all of that morning and asked many different questions. It was scary to talk to the policemen, but I knew what they were looking for, so I concentrated and tried my best not to be scared or nervous." As the police questioned her parents, Linh courageously hid some of the Bibles in her school knapsack.

When the police asked her about the contents of the knapsack, Linh simply replied, "It is books for children."

Linh Dao's father was arrested that day and sentenced to seven years of re-education through hard labor.

"When the policemen decided to take my dad away, all of my family knelt down and prayed. I prayed first, then my sister, then my mom, and last of all, my dad. I prayed that my dad would have peace and remain healthy and that my family would survive these hard times. We were all crying, but I told myself I have to face what's happening now."

Word quickly spread about the arrest, and neighbor children began to ask Linh about the crimes her father had been arrested for. She told her friends, "My father is not a criminal. He is a Christian, and I am proud of him for not wavering in his faith!"

As each day passed, Linh Dao made a mark on her wooden bookcase as she prayed for her father. She remembers, "I cried almost every single night, because I worried how my father was doing in prison and how the policemen were treating him.

"Before my dad was in prison, I was just a child. I didn't need to worry about anything. It was a lot different after my dad left. My mind got older very quickly. I told my sister that we had to help Mom do the work around the house, so she could continue to do my dad's work in the church.

"I prayed every day and every night. My faith grew very fast. I knew one thing that I had to concentrate on, and that was spending time learning from the Bible so when I grew up, I could be like my dad, sharing and preaching. When I think about this, I feel my heart burning inside me, pushing me, telling me this is the right thing to do."

Finally, after more than a year, Linh, her mother, and her sister were able to visit their father in prison. When they reached the compound, they were separated by a chain-link fence. Linh quickly discovered that she could squeeze into the prison yard through a chained gate. She ran to her father and hugged him tightly. The guards watched the little girl but, surprisingly, left her alone. *What harm can a little girl do?* they must have thought.

Little did they know! Armed with innocence and a childlike faith, children are a secret weapon against the kingdom of Satan. During that first visit to her father's prison, Linh was able to smuggle him a pen, which he used to write scriptures and sermons on cigarette paper. These "cigarette sermons" traveled from cell to cell and were instrumental in bringing many prisoners to Christ.

Linh Dao's prayers were answered. Her father was released early, before he had served all seven years of his sentence. "It was a big surprise when I came home from school one day and saw my dad had been released from prison. I ran and then gave him a big hug. We were so happy. I was proud of my family, and I wanted to yell and let the whole world know that I wasn't scared of anything, because God always protects each step I go in my life."

Linh Dao is now a teenager. She wants to follow in the footsteps of her father and be a preacher of the gospel of Jesus Christ. She knows firsthand the dangers of sharing

her faith in Communist Vietnam and remains determined
to obey Christ rather than men. In spite of a "grim future,"
she spends her time in intense Bible study.[fn4]

Don't underestimate what you – as one person – can do.
God will work through anyone – of any age – who is sub-
mitted to Him, to accomplish His will on earth. One man
or woman willing to obey God can change the destiny of
millions.

Jesus Freaks in the Bible

Jesus Freaks Hall of Fame

Long before sports associations created halls of fame for their
star players, God had one of His own. Listed in Hebrews 11,
the "Faith Hall of Fame" gives an account of men and women
who had the kind of faith Jesus said His Father is looking for.
Here's a brief rundown of the Faith Hall of Famers and what
they did to deserve a place in the biblical "Who's Who of Jesus
Freaks" (Scripture verses taken from THE MESSAGE).

ABEL: By an act of faith, Abel brought a better sacrifice to
God than Cain. It was what he believed, not what he brought,
that made the difference.

ENOCH: By an act of faith, Enoch skipped death completely
… We know on the basis of reliable testimony that before he
was taken "he pleased God." It's impossible to please God
apart from faith. And why? Because anyone who wants to
approach God must believe both that he exists and that he
cares enough to respond to those who seek him.

NOAH: By faith, Noah built a ship in the middle of dry land. He was warned about something he couldn't see, and acted on what he was told.

ABRAHAM: By an act of faith, Abraham said yes to God's call to travel to an unknown place that would become his home. When he left he had no idea where he was going.

SARAH: By faith, barren Sarah was able to become pregnant, old woman as she was at the time, because she believed the One who made a promise would do what he said.

ISAAC: By an act of faith, Isaac reached into the future as he blessed Jacob and Esau.

JACOB: By an act of faith, Jacob on his deathbed blessed each of Joseph's sons in turn, blessing them with God's blessing, not his own.

JOSEPH: By an act of faith, Joseph, while dying, prophesied the exodus of Israel, and made arrangements for his own burial.

MOSES: By faith, Moses, when grown, refused the privileges of the Egyptian royal house. He chose a hard life with God's people rather than an opportunistic soft life of sin with the oppressors. He valued suffering in the Messiah's camp far greater than Egyptian wealth because he was looking ahead, anticipating the payoff.

RAHAB: By an act of faith, Rahab, the Jericho harlot, welcomed the Israelite spies and escaped the destruction that came on those who refused to trust God.

Here the writer of Hebrews seems at a loss for words. He then writes,

> I could go on and on, but I've run out of time. There are so many more – Gideon, Barak, Samson, Jephthah, David, Samuel, the prophets … Through acts of faith, they toppled kingdoms, made justice work, took the promises for themselves. They were protected from lions, fires, and sword thrusts, turned disadvantage to advantage, won battles, routed alien armies. Women received their loved ones back from the dead. There were those who, under torture, refused to give in and go free, preferring something better: resurrection. Others braved abuse and whips, and, yes, chains and dungeons. We have stories of those who were stoned, sawed in two, murdered in cold blood; stories of vagrants wandering the earth in animal skins, homeless, friendless, powerless – the world didn't deserve them! – making their way as best they could on the cruel edges of the world.
>
> Not one of the these people, even though their lives of faith were exemplary, got their hands on what was promised. God had a better plan for us: that their faith and our faith would come together, to make one completed whole, their lives of faith not complete apart from ours.
>
> – HEBREWS 11:32–40 THE MESSAGE

Shannon

Shannon Ribeiro & Damaris Kofmehl

Heart-breaking, yet full of hope, here is a powerful, real life story of a young girl growing up on the streets of Cleveland, Ohio.

Aged 10, Shannon ran away from home to join one of Cleveland's most notorious gangs. Soon she was caught up in a world of drugs, crime and witchcraft, constantly on the run from the police with no one she could trust. Becoming increasingly violent towards other people, Shannon was convinced her heart had turned to stone. Yet she was haunted by the words of a boy at school – 'Jesus loves you'. One day those words were to cause a dramatic turnaround.

Shannon's testimony is one of hope – God is at work in the darkest of places and the hardest of hearts.

Hodder & Stoughton
ISBN: 0-3407.8648-5

Price: £6.99

£4.99 with voucher

First published in 2002 by Hodder & Stoughton
338 Euston Road, London, NW1 3BH

Chapter 5

Nicolas

On her way home, a few hundred metres from the school building, she heard someone calling out after her. When she turned around she saw a boy she didn't know rushing after her, as if he had something very important to tell her. She put him at about eleven years old, twelve at the most He looked pretty harmless, was about as tall as her, slim with blond, short-cropped hair and a pale, freckled face. His schoolbooks tucked under his left arm, a guitar slung over his right shoulder, he was hurrying to catch her up. She couldn't remember having seen the boy before. But that didn't mean much. Whoever didn't hammer very hard on the little window of her space capsule didn't exist as far as she was concerned, not even if their paths had crossed a hundred times before. There were already enough ugly spectres spinning around her head that she longed to erase from her memory. On top of that, you couldn't be expected to remember all the faces in a school with over a thousand children, and she was surprised that a boy she didn't know at all was running after her as if he had known her for ages. That had never happened to her before, and it made her curious.

'Hi,' he said, somewhat out of breath, and stretched out his hand to her, 'I'm Nicolas.'

'Hi,' growled Shannon, ignoring his hand. What do you want?'

'I saw you with that guy in the school yard.'

'And?'

'I wanted to warn you,' he said.

'Warn me? About what?'

'The Jaguars.'

Now Shannon was definitely curious. 'Why?'

'You shouldn't mess with them. Even the police are afraid of them.'

'How do you know that?'

'Everyone knows. Go out on the streets after midnight and see what happens. You'd have to have a death wish to voluntarily leave your home at night time. The gangs control the whole town. They're like a pack of wolves, and woe betide the person who strays on to their patch uninvited. He's killed in cold blood. They have a leader, a president, and whoever doesn't respect his orders is bumped off. But the wars are the worst of all.'

'What kind of wars?'

'The wars between the individual gangs. They fight over territory, and every time lots of people are injured and killed. Not even the police will intervene when they're beating each other's heads in. They wait until the following morning to gather up all the corpses. So you'd better give those people a pretty wide berth.'

'Hey, I'm not a baby any more,' said Shannon, although his description had made a real impression on her. 'I'm well able to look after myself, okay?'

'I just wanted to warn you. Those are dangerous friends you've chosen.'

'I'll choose my own friends, all right?' She quickened her pace in order to shake off the boy. But he stuck persistently on her heels, even though his guitar nearly slipped off his shoulder at the effort this entailed.

'Did you know that he carries a weapon?'

Shannon's ears pricked right up, but she nevertheless tried to remain as cool as possible.

'Listen here,' she said. 'No one in this school ever gave a damn about me. Up till now, Paul is the *only* one, the only one, get it? So don't you come up to me and talk about *friends.* I don't have any friends here, okay?'

The boy looked at her with unusual concern, and it looked as though he had something else important to get off his chest. But Shannon wouldn't let him get another word in; she turned away and crossed the road as quickly as possible.

'And as for me and Paul, that's damn all of your business, d'you hear?' She stamped off angrily, without even turning around once to look at the boy. This Nicolas had made her nervous, and not just with his information about Paul and the Jaguars. He himself had utterly thrown her, the way he spoke, the way he looked at her, the way he had followed her. Why, she kept on asking herself. Why had he done it? Why had he warned her? It needn't have bothered him a bit, not him or anybody else. Why was he sticking his nose in?

The following day as she walked along the corridor, caught up in the stream of pupils during the ten o'clock break, she saw him again. He was just coming out of the fifth-grade classroom, and at that moment he looked right at her.

'Hey, Shannon!' he called, and headed straight for her. 'There's something I forgot yesterday!' She wondered how he knew her name. He must be spying on her!

'Leave me alone, all right?' she growled.

'I thought about what you said. So I've written something down for you.' He put his hand into his pocket, pulled out a piece of paper and presented it to Shannon ceremoniously. 'Here.'

She wondered whether she should take it or simply turn around and walk away, as she had done on their first encounter. Nicolas was waiting, his hand outstretched, and his clear eyes alone seemed to encourage her to take the message. Finally she tore the note wordlessly from his hand and sank quickly back into the mass of pupils. She unfolded the paper hastily so that she could read it before Nicolas had time to catch up with her and see her reading it. The message was only two lines long, and Shannon was pretty stunned when she read it:

'Even when you think you have no friends – there is someone whose love for you knows no bounds: Jesus Christ.'

She read the message a second and then a third time, then she screwed up the note and threw it provocatively on the floor, so that Nicolas would see it when he came by. What rubbish! Jesus Christ. This Nicolas must have completely lost it. What did he know about life? Jesus Christ And what right had he to stick his nose into her life? That was just what she needed, to meet someone who thought all her problems could be solved with one single name. Jesus Christ. It would have to be him. What did he know about love? Paul was right. The injustices he had suffered screamed out to the heavens too loudly for a loving God not to have heard them and intervened. Instead, God let it all happen, horrific and merciless, and in her own life too. And then along came this Nicolas and tried to make her buy into the idea that Jesus Christ loved her.

Most of all Shannon would have liked to hide behind the stairs and wait for the boy's expression when he found the crumpled note on the floor. But then she dismissed the idea, marched out purposefully to the school yard and looked around for Paul. She found him with Terry, behind the gym. He was taking money from a girl who quickly disappeared after the deal had been done. Bob wasn't there this time.

'Hi,' said Shannon, only now realising how much she had missed the boys – Paul in particular.

'Hi, Shannon,' said Paul, putting the cash into the pocket of his jeans. Even though he only glanced over at her and didn't even smile particularly, his curt greeting nevertheless gave her the feeling that she was accepted by him, that she belonged somehow. And that made her like him all the more.

'Where's Bob?'

'Had something urgent to do,' Paul answered vaguely. 'And you? Have you made up your mind?'

'What do you mean, made up my mind?'

'To smoke a joint with me.'

Shannon shook her head.

'Definitely not?'

Another shake of the head.

Paul reached into the inner pocket of his leather jacket, and Shannon's eyes were suddenly drawn to his hips. He was armed, Nicolas had claimed. Was that true?

Terry seemed to notice her strangely searching look. 'What are you staring at?'

Shannon gave a barely perceptible jump. 'I'm not staring at anything.'

'Of course you are.' He turned to Paul. 'She was staring at your hips as if she was looking for something.'

'Perhaps this here?' asked Paul, and lifted up his ragged t-shirt for a split second. Shannon's jaw dropped in amazement. Tucked fast into his tight jeans was a revolver. Shannon didn't know what to say. Of course Nicolas had said that Paul was armed, but there was a difference between simply hearing about something and actually convincing yourself of it with your very own eyes. She had never seen a weapon before in her life, apart from on TV, of course, but that didn't count. It was a weird feeling to be standing across from someone who was carrying a weapon, especially when the person in question was a twelve- or thirteen-year-old boy.

'You knew, didn't you?' said Terry.

'No, why?' contested Shannon.

'You've been finding things out about our gang, haven't you?'

'No, not on purpose … I mean … '

'They told you you'd be better off steering dear of us. Isn't that so?'

'No, I mean yes … I mean, it wasn't like that at all … '

'How wasn't it like that?' Terry continued to dig, his arms tightly folded. Shannon was confused. She didn't know whether she was better off coming out with the truth or keeping quiet. Paul gave her a friendly shove.

'It's all right, Shannon. Lots of people here know that I've got a gun. That's no big secret. I don't really care who said it to you. I just don't want you not to trust me any more because of it. You trust me, don't you?'

Shannon nodded. 'Of course I trust you.'

'I should have told you that I carry a weapon, fair enough. I hope that's not a problem for you – the gun, I mean.'

'Of course not,' Shannon muttered, embarrassed. She would have liked to ask him why he needed a weapon, but didn't dare.

'Oh, by the way,' said Paul, changing topic abruptly and fishing a biro out of his jacket. 'If you want to meet me outside of these walls, you can get me on this number.' He took Shannon's right hand and wrote a telephone number on the back of her hand. 'Just call me and I'll come and get you, wherever you are.'

Shannon gave a mighty stare. 'You've got your own telephone?' (This was before the days when almost everyone owned a mobile phone.)

Well, not exactly. There's a public phone right in front of the factory. You just have to ask for me.'

'And what if I get someone who doesn't know you?'

'Don't worry,' Paul answered mysteriously. 'They'll know me. All Jaguars know me.'

When Shannon left the school building that afternoon Nicholas was once again hard on her heels. This boy was certainly persistent, but what he was hoping to achieve by it was a mystery to Shannon.

'What do *you* want now?' she asked, quickening her pace.

'I wanted to know if you've read it.'

'You know what? You're getting on my nerves! Why don't you go and find yourself another victim?'

'Because God loves *you*, too.'

Shannon turned towards him in irritation. 'I'm not interested in your God! God doesn't love anyone like me, okay?'

'Jesus loves everyone, Shannon.'

'Then tell him that he doesn't need to love me.'

'Won't work.'

'Why not?'

'Because I can't stop him loving you.'

Shannon stood still and gave the boy a dirty look. 'Listen up, I don't know you, and you don't know me. So quit going on about this Jesus, and just leave me alone, get it?'

She was waiting for an answer, but Nicolas said nothing. Obviously he'd finally realised that Shannon was the wrong person for his attentions, and admitted defeat. And that was just fine by Shannon. Nobody needed to interfere in her life, at least certainly not this Nicolas with his crazy ideas. The only one who had that right was Paul. It was different with Paul. He didn't bore her with things she didn't want to hear. He only came as near to her as she allowed, and that was probably what she liked so much about him.

The friendship between Paul and Shannon grew during every ten o'clock break that Paul turned up. Paul told Shannon wild stories from his life and the life of the Jaguars. And Shannon loved diving into this world that was so foreign to her, even when there was plenty that horrified her, like the sight of Bob's badly scarred stomach wound which an enemy had inflicted on him during a stabbing fight. The injury was also the reason why Bob hadn't shown his face in the school grounds for several weeks; when he showed Shannon the wound, sewn up with a good few stitches and almost healed, the girl felt pretty sick.

'Lucky he got me too low down,' he commented drily, 'otherwise I'd probably have kicked the bucket.'

Although the three Jaguars sometimes fed her pretty hair-raising stories, stories that almost stopped Shannon's heart simply listening to them, she grew more and more interested in the life of the gang. Perhaps this didn't really have so much to do with the pull of adventure, which hung almost tangibly in the air each time the three turned up behind the gym, nor with the call Of freedom, which echoed to her from the other side of the school walls as soon as the boys had climbed back over them. Perhaps her liking for the Jaguars was based rather on a simple need to belong and feel safe. She felt in safe hands with the boys, because they seemed to understand her problems.

Paul in particular showed far more empathy with her than she had ever known from anybody else. She could simply trust him with everything. She told him about the problems with her father, the arguments with her step-mother who bullied and humiliated her. Even when her classmates ganged up on her, as was so often the case, she poured her heart out to Paul, and although he couldn't take back the mocking comments of her fellow pupils, he could at least listen to her. He listened to her, yes, he even seemed to know how she felt deep inside. He knew what she was going through, because he had gone through something similar. And that bound them.

Really it was only a question of time before Shannon couldn't handle her unhappy life any longer and did some-thing stupid. And one morning it happened. It began in the English lesson. On that Tuesday morning they were dealing with the topic of friendship, and the teacher, a strict, fifty-year-old man with thick glasses and a suit that was always perfectly turned out and hair that was always correctly combed, set the pupils the task of describing an experience that revealed their relationship to a friend. When he called out Shannon's name she wanted to crawl right under the table, and while she desperately searched for a story to tell, the stares of her classmates bored right through her like sharpened knives. The teacher rocked impatiently in his chair and waited, his chin jutting forward, for her story.

'Well, Shannon? Have you nothing to tell us on the topic of friendship?'

'Yes, of course I have,' muttered Shannon, whereupon the first splutters in the back corner began and a boy whispered to his neighbour 'Shannon and friendship, she'll have to cook up something good there.'

Shannon pretended she hadn't heard the remark, and began hesitantly:

'I … I had a dose friend called Adriano, and …'

'That's a lie!' giggled a girl. 'She doesn't have a friend called Adriano.'

'She doesn't have a friend at all!' interjected another pupil.

'I thought it had to be a true story, Mr Thompson!'

'Or can you make up a friend if you don't have any?'

'Quiet!' The teacher banged the table with his fist, and the pupils fell momentarily silent. 'I don't want to hear any more comments like these in my lesson!' He looked at the culprits through his thick glasses and made a mental note of their names. 'You can carry on with your story, Shannon.'

Shannon had a lump in her throat. The hurtful comments from her fellow pupils made her want to cry, but she pulled herself together and swallowed her feelings. It would only have given them more reason to mock her.

'What are you going to tell?' whispered a girl behind her in her ear. 'You haven't got any friends!'

'Quiet!!!' Once again Mr. Thomas banged on the desk, and this time he looked sharply at the girl behind Shannon. 'I thought I'd made myself clear, Marianne!' Marianne's name too went on his black list.

'You haven't got any friends!' repeated the girl, so softly this time that the teacher no longer heard. Just one more word, and Shannon would have turned around and punched Marianne. But she pursed her lips, curled up her fists under the table and forced herself to remain calm, even if it was difficult.

In the ten o'clock break she sat, as always, on the stone bench and twisted her dark brown hair between her fingers, staring off into empty space. When Paul arrived she was so far away that he had to call her twice before she finally reacted.

'Shannon,' said the boy, sitting down next to her, 'what's happened?'

'They showed me up,' she said weakly. 'The whole class had a great laugh. They said I haven't got any friends.'

'You know full well that's not true. You've got me, for example, a real Jaguar, member of the most feared gang in Cleveland. One word from me and a hundred Jaguars will make these cocky bigmouths wet themselves like little babies.'

A tear rolled down Shannon's cheek, and she wiped it away discreetly. Paul's words of encouragement were no comfort to her this time. She was more deeply wounded than that. Paul put his arm around her shoulder.

'Hey, girl, didn't I tell you: school here just isn't your thing. How long are you going to let it go on for? How much longer are they going to be allowed to walk all over you? Give this snobby school the finger and make up your mind at last! Make up your mind, Shannon!'

'What for? If I don't go to school any more, my father will come and beat the living daylights out of me.'

'Then give your father the finger as well! Just because he brought you into this wretched world doesn't mean you have to spend your life giving in to him! It's *your* life! Do you want to wait until he beats you to death?'

Shannon gave a deep sigh and fell silent. When the school bell rang, Paul got up, and with the words: 'You know where to find me,' he left.

Shannon was in no hurry to get to class. She knew only too well what cynical comments and looks awaited her there. But something else was waiting for her, too: on her small desk lay a folded-up piece of paper. Somebody must have put it there during break time. She unfolded the squared paper, and as soon as she had read the short message her pulse hit 180. That was just what she needed! As if she didn't have enough to put up with! She crumpled the paper hastily into her fist and marched, her mind already made up, in the direction of the door. That was too much! The final straw! She didn't have to put up with that! She bumped straight into Mr. Thompson in the doorway.

'What's your rush, then?'

Shannon stormed past him, her head bowed like a bull preparing for attack, although her target wasn't a red rag but rather the door at the other end of the corridor.

'Hey!' called out her teacher in surprise. 'What's all this about, Shannon? Come back here!'

Shannon didn't take any notice of him. Her left hand was curled up into a fist, and her nostrils were flaring in anger.

'Shannon, it's time for class!'

Shannon marched on, heading straight for the fifth-grade room, and when she had reached the door she tore it open and landed right in the middle of the lesson. The teacher was standing at the blackboard, and looked at Shannon in as much amazement as the pupils.

'You should knock before you enter.'

Shannon lifted her head, cast a searching glance over the class and then headed for a blond-haired boy in the second row. And before anybody had time to react, she punched him so hard in the chest that he fell backwards while still sitting in his chair. Then she threw the crumpled note into his face, and shouted almost hysterically: 'I don't need your stupid messages, okay!'

The fifth graders sat in their places with eyes open wide in dismay, not daring to move. The teacher had dropped the chalk. She put her hand to her mouth and looked equally out of her depth. Nicolas tried to pick himself up from the floor, but Shannon was on him in a flash and began throwing punches with her fists.

'I don't want you interfering in my life! Get it?! You don't even know me! I don't want to have anything to do with you, is that clear?! I hate you! I hate you! You and your Jesus! I hate you both!'

Two boys who didn't want to sit by any longer and see one of their fellow pupils being beaten up by a girl tried to tear Shannon off Nicolas – with the result that they lost their balance and joined him on the floor. A few girls circled around, a few boys began to whistle encouragingly. The pupils got up from their chairs and formed a circle around the battle scene, while the teacher stood rooted to the spot by the blackboard and called out for them to put an end to this nonsense.

Now Mr Thompson turned up in the doorway as well, and when he saw the chaos he turned right around to call the headmaster.

The boys received a few hefty kicks and punches when they tried once more to pull the maddened girl off her fellow pupil, and even when two of them held Shannon by the arms she kicked out with her legs so wildly that she knocked all the books and pens from the desks standing within reach. Only when a third boy joined in did they manage to put the ten-year-old out of action. Nicolas felt his nose carefully. It was bleeding.

'That's what you deserve!' shouted Shannon, spitting in his direction. 'That's what you're worth to me, get it? And your Jesus too! Tell the people in the church about Jesus, but not me. Not me, d'you hear?!'

Nicolas pulled himself up with effort, planted himself exhaustedly back on to the chair and wiped the blood from his nose, countering Shannon's look all the time with his bright eyes – without saying a word.

'What's all this actually about?' asked a girl quietly.

'Haven't a clue,' said another, shrugging her shoulders. 'But I don't care anyway. The main thing is, we've got out of maths.'

'I think it's to do with this note,' said a third girl, bending down to pick up the crumpled piece of paper from the floor. It was smeared with blood.

'Let's see,' said the first girl, and carefully unfolded it. The girls put their heads together while Shannon carried on cursing in the background, the teacher kept on trying to demand some sort of order, and the angry voices of Mr Thompson and the headmaster sounded in the corridor.

The message was a mere ten words long, and with the best will in the world the girls couldn't understand why these words had given rise to such chaos. It was only a few words, written with blue ink on a scrap of squared paper. Just words.

'I just want to tell you: Jesus Christ loves you!'

The girls shook their heads in disbelief.

'What rubbish.'

'Typical Nicolas.'

'And she went for him just because of that. She's crazy.' One of the girls crumpled up the scrap of paper again and threw it out of the open window. It landed somewhere on the tarmacked yard, so small and inoffensive that it was trodden to pieces by the first crowd of noisy school-children who ran over it during the next break time. It was only a few words, after all. Just words.

Unquenchable Worshipper

Matt Redman

This book is about a kind of worshipper – unquenchable, undivided and unpredictable. On a quest to bring glory and pleasure to God, these worshippers will not allow themselves to be distracted or defeated. They long for their hearts, lives and songs to be the kind of offerings God is looking for.

Sharing observances and insight drawn from his own vast experience as a worship leader, Matt Redman takes a refreshing and original look at worshipping God.

Kingsway
ISBN:0-8547.6995-1

Price:£4.99

£3.99 with voucher

First published in 2001 by Kingsway Publications
26-28 Lottbridge Drove, Eastbourne,
East Sussex, BN23 6NT

1

The Unquenchable Worshipper

Enter, the unquenchable worshipper. This world is full of fragile loves – love that abandons, love that fades, love that divorces, love that is self-seeking. But the unquenchable worshipper is different. From a heart so amazed by God and His wonders, burns a love that will not be extinguished. It survives any situation and lives through any circumstance. It will not allow itself to be quenched, for that would heap insult on the love it lives in response to.

These worshippers gather beneath the shadow of the cross, where an undying devotion took the Son of God to His death. Alive now in the power of His resurrection, they respond to such an outpouring with an unquenchable offering of their own.

The Bible is full of unquenchable worshippers – people who refused to be dampened, discouraged or distracted in their quest to glorify God. I love the heart attitude of the prophet Habakkuk, who decided he would choose to respond to God's worth, no matter how bleak a season he found himself in:

> Though the fig-tree does not bud and there are no grapes on the vines, though the olive crop fails and the fields produce no food, though there are no sheep in the pen and no cattle in the

stalls, yet I will rejoice in the Lord, I will be joyful in God my Saviour.

(Habakkuk 3:17–18)

In Acts 16, Paul and Silas also resolve to overcome less than favourable conditions and worship God. Sitting in their jail cell you would have forgiven them if they weren't in the mood for singing. They'd been unjustly arrested, beaten, 'severely' flogged, and thrown into the deepest part of the prison, with their feet in stocks. Yet, somehow, Paul and Silas found it in themselves to sing out praise to God. Refusing to let their souls be dampened, they worshipped with everything they had left.

Most of us don't own fig trees, and haven't been in prison for being a Christian, but the principle is the same for us as it was for Habakkuk, Paul and Silas – we can always find a reason to praise. Situations change for better and for worse, but God's worth never changes.

I recently heard the story of Fanny Crosby, the American hymn writer of the nineteenth century. She described a life-changing incident that happened to her as a baby:

When about six weeks old I was taken sick and my eyes grew very weak and those who had charge of me poulticed my eyes. Their lack of knowledge and skill destroyed my sight forever. As I grew older they told me I should never see the faces of my friends, the flowers of the field, the blue of the skies, or the golden beauty of the stars ... Soon I learned what other children possessed, but I made up my mind to store away a little jewel in my heart which I called 'Content'.[1]

In fact Fanny Crosby was only eight years old when she wrote this song:

O what a happy soul am I!
Although 1 cannot see,
I am resolved that in this world
Contented I will be.

How many blessings I enjoy,
That other people don't.
To weep and sigh because I'm blind,
I cannot, and I won't.[2]

And this contented worshipper went on to write around
8,000 hymns of praise. Those thousands of songs were simply the result of a fire that burned in her heart for Jesus and
could not be put out. Someone once asked her, 'Fanny, do
you wish you had not been blinded?' She replied, in typical
style, 'Well, the good thing about being blind is that the
very first face I'll see will be the face of Jesus.'

Many might have chosen the path of bitterness and
complaint as their response to God, but she chose the path
of contentment and praise. The choice between these two
paths faces us each day, with every situation that's thrown
our way. Bitterness dampens and eventually destroys love
for God. It eats away at the statement 'God is love' and tells
us He is not faithful. But contentment does the opposite: it
fuels the heart with endless reasons to praise God.

And there *are* endless reasons to praise Him. I once
heard Pete Waterman (of production team Stock, Aitken
and Waterman) talking about love songs in the world of
pop music. He cynically suggested that you can write only
four songs – 'I love you', 'I hate you', 'Go away' and 'Come
back'. I'm thankful, as someone who writes worship songs,
that there's a lot more songwriting material to get your
heart into than that! I'll never be able to think, 'Right,

that's God pretty much wrapped up … what shall I write about next?' The brightness of His glory and the wonders of His heart will no doubt have us pouring out new songs for all eternity.

At the end of Song of Songs comes a fantastic declaration of unquenchable worship:

> … love is as strong as death, its jealousy unyielding as the grave. It burns like blazing fire, like a mighty flame. Many waters cannot quench love; rivers cannot wash it away.
>
> (Song of Songs 8:6–7)

Too often my worship is tamed by the complications and struggles of this world. But I long to be in a place where my fire for God cannot be quenched or washed away, even by the mightiest rivers of opposition – a worship which can never be extinguished.

Fire extinguishers work by removing one of the three things needed to keep a fire ablaze: heat, oxygen and fuel. So, in other words, there are three main ways to put a fire out: cool the burning material with water (or some other such substance), cut off the oxygen or cut off the supply of fuel.

And I think there's a parallel here with our hearts of worship. We long to be a people whose hearts burn for God, but if we're not careful there are ways we can lose something of that fire.

First, just as water can put a fire out, so too the pressures and the trials of this life can dampen our hearts of worship. It's so easy in a time of hardship to 'cool off' a bit, and lose that sense of wonder and trust. We ask why God would let such things happen to us, and we wind down our worship, kidding ourselves that we'll start up again when things are better. Or maybe we don't 'feel' like worshipping any more, so we don't. I've seen many worshippers thrown off course by difficult situations. But I've also seen people who have endured even more difficult situations and emerged with their hearts of worship burning as strongly as ever, if not stronger.

There is a kind of worshipper who 'always trusts, always hopes, always perseveres', and who gets through the storms of life with a heart still blazing. Sometimes it comes down to a simple choice. We may be hard pressed on every side, weary and not able to sense God. But then a choice faces us – to fix our eyes on the circumstances, or to cling on to God and choose to worship Him, even when it hurts. The heart of God *loves* the offerings of a persevering worshipper. Though overwhelmed by many troubles, they are even more overwhelmed by the beauty of God.

The second way to extinguish a fire is to cut off the oxygen. In worship terms this means to quench the Holy Spirit, It's plain from the Bible that we worship by the Holy Spirit (Philippians 3:3), but it's also clear that the Holy Spirit can be grieved. Ephesians 4:30 urges us: '… do not grieve the Holy Spirit of God.' Then it tells us some of the ways not to grieve Him: 'Get rid of all bitterness, rage and anger.' The implications of this are huge. Take our church services, for example. We talk a lot about 'Spirit-led worship', but if we truly want to be led by the Holy Spirit, we need to make sure we're keeping in step with Him in our everyday lives. As a worship leader this is a challenging and even scary thought. I need to make sure that I'm making my life an appropriate dwelling place for Him. An unquenchable, burning worshipper needs to be full of the Holy Spirit.

The third way of stopping a fire is to cut off the fuel it thrives on. If you've ever watched TV footage of a forest fire, you may have noticed the fire fighters burn or chop away a whole section of forest so that when the fire reaches that place it cannot spread any further.

The revelation of God is the fuel for the fire of our worship. And there is always more fuel for the fire. When we open the eyes of our heart, God's revelation comes flying at us from so many different angles. He's revealed Himself to us in creation, throughout the history of His people, and overwhelmingly at the cross. And to this day, every breath we breathe is a reminder of our Maker, and every hour holds the possibility of living in His presence. We simply need to keep putting ourselves in a place where we're likely to receive this revelation. The heart of worship is fuelled by essential things such as reading God's word, praying to Him and going to church to share fellowship together. There are other ways too, such as getting out into nature – the ocean, mountains, or just a field – to soak our souls in the wonder of our Creator.

Romans 1:20 tells us there's no excuse for those who don't believe, as God has revealed who He is to everyone through all He's created.

My wife, Beth, and I have just had our first child – a beautiful little daughter called Maisey. I wonder how people could ever deny the existence of God after having witnessed the birth of a baby. The nine months leading up to Maisey's birth were a fascinating time and spoke volumes to us of the wonder of God and His creation. Ultrasound scans gave a fantastic insight into her growth and development. How could it be that this tiny baby was living and kicking with its little heart beating inside the body of my wife? How could it be so well formed, with miniature fingernails, at such an early stage? I was amazed at the goodness of God to us, and with the wonder of what He had made. Every little movement and kick I felt when I placed my hand on Beth's stomach was the revelation of God to me.

So often when my worship has dried up it's because I haven't been fuelling the fire. I haven't set aside any time to soak myself under the showers of God's revelation. Often time is the key factor. But if we can find space to soak ourselves in God's word, His presence, His creation, and spend time with other believers, then we'll find that the revelation floods back into our lives, and our hearts will respond with a blaze of worship once more.

Earlier in this chapter I mentioned worshipping God even in our darkest hour. But that doesn't mean we're to be 'shiny, happy' Christians, living in unreality, and not admitting when there are things wrong in our lives. There's definitely a place for brokenness and weeping in worship, but there's a right way and a wrong way to express this.

When we pour out our heart-cries to God, they mustn't ever become a criticism of who He is. Apparently, about 70% of the Psalms are laments – in other words, songs of sorrow and crying out.[3] A true lament never challenges or questions the worth of God. Instead, it knows that His goodness and greatness are the only hope for a bleak situation. Even at our lowest ebb there should be an underlying trust, and therefore worship. It's a precious song of praise that can overcome any obstacle, and rise from the heart of the troubled believer to the very heart of God. Such songs cry out, 'Even in my darkest hour I can still glimpse the brightness of Your worth, and the goodness of Your heart. I am in a desperate state, but no circumstance or trial could ever overshadow You.' It is praise that costs, even hurts. But sacrifices often hurt.

The Psalms have in fact been described as 'praise in the presence and absence of God'.[4] In other words, a worship which survives every situation, whether God seems close or nowhere to be found. These laments are deep cries to God from a place of despair. But is that really 'worship', or is it simply 'complaining'? In one sense, yes, they are complaints. These petitions to God are the worship songs of a broken people. But almost without exception they also display an underlying confidence and trust in God, and so are truly worship. As B. W. Anderson explains: '... the laments are really expressions of praise – praise offered in a minor key in the confidence that Yahweh is faithful ...'[5]

I love Psalm 89 for that reason. At first glance it doesn't look like a lament at all. Starting with the optimistic lyric, 'I will sing of the Lord's great love for ever', it seems to be the worship song of an untroubled heart. But that isn't the case. When we get to verse 49 we discover the struggle going on in the Psalmist's soul: 'O Lord, where is your former great love, which in your faithfulness you swore to David?'

Hasn't he just contradicted himself? He seems to thank God for His great love and then wonder where it is? Exactly! At present he cannot see or feel the measure of God's love, yet he knows it to be as real and strong as it ever was. He's a man who's looked over God's track record and found it to be perfect. And so he rises up with an unquenchable song of faith and trust.

Jesus Himself used the words from the Psalms of lament as He suffered the cruelty of the cross. In agony of heart, mind, body and spirit, He cried out, 'My God, my God, why have you forsaken me?' from Psalm 22. It is a cry of torment, yet of strangely submissive devotion. The Son of God then breathes His last with a verse from Psalm 31 – another lament psalm: 'Into your hands I commit my spirit' (v.5). Amazingly, at this point of utter torment, Jesus is offering up the common worship songs of His day. And in so doing He becomes an inspiration to us. Whatever trials lie ahead in this life, unquenchable worshippers are found with a song of undying worship on their lips.

Notes

1. Fanny Crosby, retold by S. Trevena Jackson, *This Is My Story, This Is My Song* (Emerald House, 1997).
2. *Ibid.*
3. Eugene Peterson, *The Message of David* (Marshall Pickering, 1997).
4. Bernard W. Anderson, *Out of the Depths* (Westminster John Knox Press, 2000).
5. *Ibid.*

Incomparable Christ

John Stott

Jesus Christ has been the dominant figure in the history of Western culture for two thousand years. His birth is the pivot of our calendar. He is the focus of Scripture: as Luther declared, 'the entire Scripture deals only with Christ everywhere'. He is the heart of mission, the message that countless Christians cross land and sea, continents and cultures, to deliver.

John Stott looks at the New Testament witness, at the way the church has portrayed Christ down the centuries and at the influence Christ has had on individuals over the last two thousand years, in this book which ultimately asks what Christ should mean to us today.

Inter-Varsity Press
ISBN: 0-8511-1485-7

Price: £8.99

£6.99 with voucher

First published in 2001 by Inter-Varsity Press
38 De Montfort Street, Leicester
LE1 7GP

Christ the complete fulfilment: Justin Martyr

The prophets and the philosophers

The church father who expressed this sense of fulfilment most forcefully was probably Justin Martyr (c. 100 c. 165). Justin was born of pagan parents in Samaria. Intellectually precocious, his search for the truth began during his youth. He delved successively into the philosophies of the Stoics, Aristotle, Pythagoras and Plato. But he found neither truth nor peace. Then one day, in God's good providence, near the sea at Ephesus he met an old man, who introduced him to the Old Testament prophets, and so to Christ. After his conversion he continued to wear the philosopher's robe, travelled on foot to a number of leading cities to teach, and founded a Christian school in Rome.

Justin became the greatest Christian apologist of the second century. He resolved to reconcile faith and reason, to harmonize Hebrew scripture and Greek philosophy, and to defend Christianity against misrepresentation and slander. His *First Apology* was addressed to Emperor Antoninus Pius, and to his adopted son and his successor,

Marcus Aurelius. His Second Apology, addressed to the
Roman senate, is a short appendix to the First, and was
prompted by the unjust persecution of Christians. Justin's
third and longest work is his *Dialogue with Trypho a Jew,* who
was a learned Rabbi. It has been described as 'the first elab-
orate exposition of the reasons for regarding Christ as the
Messiah of the Old Testament, and the first systematic
attempt to exhibit the false position of the Jews in regard to
Christianity'.[1] With courtesy and patience Justin witnessed to Christ in all the Scriptures (though resorting
sometimes to fanciful allegory), proclaiming the gospel of
Christ crucified and risen. He concluded with a moving
appeal to Trypho and his friends to believe in Christ: 'Say
no evil thing, my brothers, against him that was crucified
… Assent, therefore, and pour no ridicule on the Son of
God.'[2]

In about AD 165 Justin was denounced as a Christian, he
refused to offer sacrifice to the gods, and went to a martyr's
death with calm and courage.

'Jesus Christ the complete fulfilment' is the phrase I am
suggesting as a summary of Justin's theology. In his *First
Apology* he marshalled many Old Testament prophecies
(with a particular fondness for Moses, the Psalms and
Isaiah) which pointed to Christ.\ His knowledge of the
Old Testament was phenomenal. But he also believed that
at least to some extent Christianity is the embodiment of
all that is best in Greek philosophy. So at his conversion,
although he renounced paganism, he did not renounce
philosophy. How is it, then, that the philosophers came to
know the truths they knew? It was partly that (so he
claimed) Plato borrowed from Moses and the prophets.
But it was also that the divine Logos, who had been in the
world from the beginning and became fully incarnate in

Jesus Christ, was distributed by the divine Sower everywhere. Thus 'there seem to be seeds of truth among all men'.[3] For example, the Stoics' moral teaching was admirable 'on account of the *logos spermatikos* (rational seed or seed of reason) implanted in every race of men'.[4] This applies to all the philosophers. 'For all the writers were able to see realities darkly through the sowing of the implanted seed that was in them.'[5] In consequence, 'those who lived in accordance with reason are Christians, even though they were declared godless [in relation to the pagan gods], such as among the Greeks Socrates ... and among the barbarians [i.e. non-Greeks] Abraham ... Elijah ... and many others'. For 'those who lived by reason, and those who so live now, are Christians ...',[6] that is, Christians before Christ.

Thus the prophets and the philosophers, though in differing degrees, bore witness to Christ, and what they wrote finds its fulfilment in Christ. One is filled with admiration for the breadth of Justin's vision, for his determination to claim for Christ everything that is true, wherever it might be found, and for his gracious and generous spirit.

Perhaps then it is ungenerous and ungracious of me to add that I wish he had developed a more obviously biblical basis for his theme. His references to *logos* (word or reason) could well have led him to the Prologue to John's Gospel. For John 1:9 seems to summarize Justin's conviction: 'The true light that gives light to every man was coming into the world.' That is, before he 'came' in the incarnation, he 'was coming', and is coming still, giving light to everybody. It is not saving light (as Justin knew), yet it is light, so that everything beautiful, good and true, wherever found, originates in the Logos, 'the true light', Jesus Christ.

Notes

[1] Introductory note to the *First Apology* of Justin Martyr, in A. Roberts and J. Donaldson (eds.), *The Ante-Nicene Fathers* (1885); Eeerdmans, n.d.), vol. 1, p. 160.
[2] Martyr, *First Apology*, para. 137
[3] Ibid., para. 44
[4] Martyr, *Second Apology*, paras. 8, 13
[5] Ibid., para 13
[6] Martyr, *First Apology*, para. 46

Christ the heavenly bridegroom: Bernard of Clairvaux

Christian mysticism

Christian mysticism came to full flower in Europe between the twelfth and the fourteenth centuries. It focused on Jesus Christ as the lover, indeed the bridegroom, of the Christian soul, and Bernard of Clairvaux (1090–1153) was the most popular exponent of it.

In spite of a natural shyness, and his constant ill-health due to his austere self-discipline, Bernard was a born leader, endowed with many and varied gifts. He preached and wrote with considerable eloquence, and was strongly committed to the reform of the monasteries. He was nevertheless drawn into ecclesiastical politics and exerted an enormous influence on successive popes, bishops and councils, and on the whole church. During the last two turbulent decades of his life he was widely regarded as 'the conscience of all Europe'.

At the same time, he was a diligent student of Scripture and an orthodox theologian. Indeed, his Christ-centred message was an essential aspect of his protest against an over-emphasis on the intellect and against the institutionalism and nominalism of the medieval church.

Bernard's best-known work is probably his *Sermons on the Canticle of Canticles.* He was by no means the first scholar to develop an allegorical interpretation of the Song of Songs. Defending its inclusion in the Old Testament canon, the celebrated Jewish Rabbi Aqiba said: 'all the Scriptures are holy, but the Song of Songs is the Holy of Holies'.[1] There had also been Christian commentaries on the Song by early church fathers, one by Origen in the third century, and another by Gregory of Nyssa in the fourth. But Bernard's sermons were the most widely read and cherished.[2] He was known as 'the mellifluous doctor', and in Luther's opinion 'Bernard surpasses all the other doctors of the church'.[3]

During the last eighteen years of his life (1135–1153) Bernard preached eighty-six sermons on the Song of Songs, although even then he covered only the first two chapters of the book. In no sense was he writing a commentary, but rather a series of meditations for advanced believers who were 'ripe for the mystical nuptials of the Heavenly Bridegroom'.[4] His first eight sermons all had the same text, which is the second verse of the Song, namely: 'Let him kiss me with the kisses of his mouth.'

Needless to say, his treatment of it was a fanciful allegorization. For example, he elaborated three kisses (of the feet, the hand and the mouth), which symbolize three stages of the soul's progress towards perfection. To kiss Christ's feet is to prostrate ourselves before him in humble penitence, like Mary in the gospel story. This is the beginning of conversion. To kiss Christ's hand is to acknowledge that he is the giver of all good gifts, and that our relationship to him is based on his mercy, not on our merit. Few, however, reach the third kiss. This is 'the supreme kiss', when with fear and trembling we venture to raise ourselves 'to that divinely glorious mouth' and so enjoy the kiss of loving union with God, Father, Son and Holy Spirit.[5] Summed up in the declaration that 'my love is mine and I am his' (2:16), it expresses the ultimate union of the soul with God for which the mystic longs.

Many of us have probably been brought up to believe that Bernard's personal devotion to Christ was best expressed in his hymns. I am thinking specially of the following: 'Jesus, the very thought of thee / With sweetness fills the breast', and 'Jesus, the very thought is sweet / In that dear name all heart-joys meet', and

> Jesus, thou joy of loving hearts,
> Thou fount of life, thou light of men,
> From the best bliss that earth imparts
> We turn unfilled to thee again.

Although these hymns have been attributed for a long time to Bernard, hymnologists are now telling us that there is no evidence for this attribution. They are content to say simply that the hymns' Latin originals go back to the twelfth century. But at least an authority like Archbishop Trench could write that, if Bernard did not compose them, 'it is not easy to guess who could have written them', for 'they bear profoundly the stamp of his mind, being only inferior in beauty to his prose'.[6]

Before we leave Bernard of Clairvaux and his mystical attachment to Christ, we need to ask two questions.

First, what is the nature of Christian mysticism? Because the language of mysticism is used in Hinduism, Buddhism, Taoism, Neoplatonism, Judaism and Islam, as well as in Christianity, it is too readily assumed that to be a 'mystic' means the same thing in all religions. But this is not so. To be sure, everybody means by 'mysticism' some rather ill-defined experience like 'union with the ultimate'. But there is at least one fundamental difference between eastern mysticism and Christian mysticism. The objective of eastern mystics is to lose their individuality through absorption in the divine, like a drop of water becoming dissolved in the ocean. In Christian mysticism, however, the individual believer retains his or her identity. For God has created us with our own unique individuality, and has redeemed us so that we may become even more, not less, our true selves. Our destiny is not to lose ourselves, but by losing ourselves to find ourselves. To be 'in Christ' (a favourite expression of Paul's) is to be so intimately and organically united to him as to share his life. Jesus prayed that his followers might be 'one' just as he and the Father are one (John 17:21–23). But the three persons of the Trinity, although one, are yet eternally distinct.

The second question which needs to be asked is whether it is legitimate to use the Song of Songs as an allegory of the love between Christ and the Christian soul. In general, it is legitimate to use allegory to illustrate, but not to substantiate, a truth. That is, if a doctrine or duty is already established by the plain meaning of a biblical passage, then it is legitimate to use allegory to illustrate this truth. Thus Scripture teaches plainly and often that God and his people are committed to each other in a covenant of love. Therefore it is legitimate to use the Song of Songs, which expresses the love of bridegroom and bride for each other, in order to illustrate this truth.

In particular, the Song of Songs has been individualized too often and made to set forth the private and personal love which unites God and the individual. By contrast, the two prophets of divine love (Hosea and Jeremiah) paint a picture of God's love for his covenant people. For example, promises like 'I will betroth you to me for ever' are not spoken to individuals but to the unfaithful nation (Hos. 2:19). Similarly in the New Testament Paul writes that 'Christ loved the church and gave himself up for her' (Eph. 5:25). True, Paul could also write that 'the Son of God … loved *me* and gave himself for *me*' (Gal. 2:20, my emphasis), but such flashes of individualism are rare, perhaps because of the risk of spiritual eroticism, a risk which – at least in language – the Christian mystics have not always managed to avoid.

Notes

[1] Quoted by M.H.Pope in The Song of Songs, in the Anchor Bible Commentary (Doubleday, 1977), p. 19.
[2] *St Bernard's Sermons on the Canticle of Canticles* (Browne & Nelson, 1920), translated from the original Latin, in two volumes.
[3] Ibid., vol. 1, p. xiv.
[4] Ibid., vol. 1, p. 9.
[5] Ibid., vol. 1, p. 1–67.
[6] 'Bernard of Clairvaux' in J. Julian (ed.), *A Dictionary of Hymnology* (John Murray, rev. ed. 1907).

Christ the global Lord:
Mission in the twentieth century

From Edinburgh 1910 to Lausanne 1974

It was the risen Jesus who made the great claim that all authority had been given to him in heaven and on earth
(Matt. 28:18). In consequence, the church has always borne
witness to his universal lordship. For God has super-exalted
him, and given him the name above every other name (that
is, the rank beyond every other rank), in order that every
knee should bow to him and every tongue confess him
'Lord' (Phil. 2:9–11). This is the fundamental basis of the
world-wide mission of the church, as has been well illus-
trated in the twentieth century.

In 1910 the World Missionary Conference was con-
vened in Edinburgh, under the chairmanship of John R.
Mott. It had been carefully prepared for over a period of
eighteen months by eight international commissions,
whose printed reports had been read in advance by the
1,200 or so delegates. John Mott himself claimed that in its
plan, personnel, spirit and promise it was 'the most significant gathering ever held in the interest of the world's
evangelization'.[1]

John Mott's book, *The Decisive Hour of Christian Missions,* exudes the euphoria that had been generated during the conference. In the light of spiritual awakenings in South East Asia, mass movements in India, the rapid progress of the gospel in Africa, the weakening hold of other religions and 'the rising spiritual tide in the non-Christian world',[2] Mott wrote of abundant ground for hopefulness and confidence'.[3] Indeed, 'the way is unmistakably being prepared for the acceptance of Christianity by large masses of the people in many lands'.[4] And using what we would regard as an unfortunate military metaphor, Mott continued: 'On the world-wide battlefield of Christianity ... victory is assured ...'[5]

The delegates left Edinburgh elated and inspired. They were under no illusions about the immensity of the task. They knew that there were still about 1,000 million non-Christians in the world, no more than one-fifth of whom had heard clearly about Christ. But they were determined. They agreed with John Mott that 'it is the church's duty to see that this long-standing reproach is completely removed'.[6] Also, 'it is high time that the church deliberately and resolutely attack some of the hitherto almost impregnable fortresses'.[7] They believed (somewhat naïvely) that under the influence of Christ other religions would gradually disappear, like the old gods of Greece and Rome.

Who could have guessed that within the next few years this missionary emphasis would have evaporated almost entirely? There were two main reasons. First came the horrors of the First World War in 1914. Not only were Christians divided by the conflict, but almost all international enterprises were put on hold. And when post-war reconstruction began, the world had changed and moved on.

Secondly, the spread of liberal theology between the wars called into question the content of the gospel and undermined people's confidence in it. This was very evident at the next two missionary conferences – at Jerusalem (1928) and Tambaram outside Madras (1938). Whereas at Edinburgh the mood had been confident, at Jerusalem and Tambaram it was largely diffident and hesitant.

At Jerusalem (1928) a comparatively small group of about 200 gathered, although it was notable that about fifty of them belonged to what were now called the younger churches. Their broad agenda therefore included relations between the older and the younger churches, in addition to such topics as race relations, urban and rural questions, religious education and the menace of secularism. Theologically, relativism reigned. Christianity could no longer be regarded as either unique or final. William Temple saved the conference from disaster by drafting the 'Message', which included the epigram about the gospel that 'either it is true for all, or it is not true at all'.

The World Missionary Conference at Tambaram (1938) brought about 500 delegates together, and the representatives of the younger churches were equal in numbers to, and on an equal footing with, those from the older churches. But the most noteworthy feature of Tambaram was the sharp encounter between William E. Hocking and Hendrik Kraemer. Hocking was Professor of Philosophy at Harvard. His book *Re-thinking Missions* had been published in 1932, so that conference participants had had time to peruse it. In it the old missionary certainties had gone. So had any exclusive claim for Christ. Seeking conversions was frowned upon, and should be replaced by seeking the best in all religions. The ultimate goal of mission was said to be the emergence of a world fellowship of faiths.

Hocking's sparring partner at Tambaram was Hendrik Kraemer, a Dutch Reformed layman and seasoned linguist-missionary in Indonesia. He had been invited to write a book for the conference. It was published in 1938 under the title *The Christian Message in a non-Christian World*. Influenced by Karl Barth (whose assault on liberalism in his commentary on Romans had appeared in 1919), he defended what he called 'biblical realism'. He maintained that there was a radical discontinuity between God's unique revelation in Jesus Christ and all human religion.

This debate continues today and has by no means been resolved. A year after Tambaram, the Second World War broke out, and again ecumenical relationships were largely suspended until it was over. Then in 1948 the first assembly of the World Council of Churches took place in Amsterdam, and in 1961, at its third assembly in New Delhi, the World Council of Churches and the International Missionary Council were amalgamated. Assurances were given that the merger would bring mission to the forefront of the World Council's agenda. But this has not happened. Instead, the World Council has continued to drift away from the biblical gospel.

Not that all conciliar leaders have followed. For example, Visser't Hooft, the first General Secretary of the World Council of Churches, wrote in his book *No Other Name*: 'It is high time that Christians should rediscover that the very heart of their faith is that Jesus Christ did not come to make a contribution to the religious storehouse of mankind, but that in him God reconciled the world to himself.'[8]

More striking still is this forthright statement by the late Bishop Lesslie Newbigin:

> The contemporary embarrassment about the missionary movement of the previous century is not, as we like to think, evidence that we have become more humble. It is, I fear, much more clearly evidence of a shift in belief. It is evidence that we are less ready to affirm the uniqueness, the centrality, the decisiveness of Jesus Christ as universal Lord and Saviour, the Way by following whom the world is to find its true goal, the Truth by which every other claim to truth is to be tested, the Life in whom alone life in its fulness is to be found.[9]

The fact is that during the last quarter of the twentieth century the missionary initiative passed from the World Council to the Lausanne movement, which was launched by Dr Billy Graham. The International Congress on World Evangelization was held in Lausanne, Switzerland, in 1974. Some 2,700 participants (50% from the developing world) came together from 150 nations, and after nine days of hectic activity endorsed the Lausanne Covenant which, according to a theologian from Asia, may prove to be 'the most significant ecumenical confession on evangelism that the church has ever produced'. It is all the more important because its background is that of 'pluralism' which insists on the equal legitimacy of every religion.

The Covenant consists of fifteen paragraphs, and I quote here from the third paragraph on 'The Uniqueness and Universality of Christ'. This is how the church proclaims 'Jesus Christ the global Lord':

> We affirm that there is only one Saviour and only one Gospel ... We recognize that all men have some knowledge of God

through his general revelation in nature. But we deny that this can save, for men suppress the truth by their unrighteousness. We also reject as derogatory to Christ and the Gospel every kind of syncretism and dialogue which implies that Christ speaks equally through all religions and ideologies. Jesus Christ, being himself the only God-man, who gave himself as the only ransom for sinners, is the only mediator between God and man. There is no other name by which we must be saved … Jesus Christ has been exalted above every other name; we long for the day when every knee shall bow to him and every tongue shall confess him Lord.'[10]

Notes

[1] J.R.Mott, *The Decisive Hour of Christian Missions* (Student Volunteer Movement, 1910), p. v.
[2] Ibid., p. 94.
[3] Ibid., p. 69.
[4] Ibid., p. 39.
[5] Ibid., p. 69.
[6] Ibid., pp. 100–101.
[7] Ibid., p. 106.
[8] Viser't Hooft, No Other Name (SCM, 1963), p. 95.
[9] *The International Bulletin of Missionary Research* (April, 1988). Published by the Overseas Ministries Study Centre, New Haven, Connecticut, USA.
[10] Stott (ed.), *Making Christ Known*, p. 16.

Mark for Everyone

Tom Wright

On the very first occasion when someone stood up in public to tell people about Jesus, he made it very clear: this message is for everyone. That is as true today as it was then.

This book will introduce you to the shortest and sharpest stories about Jesus. Many people think Mark's gospel was the first to be written, and certainly it has all the zip and punch of a quick, hasty story that's meant to grab you by the collar and make you face the truth about Jesus, about God and about yourself. So here it is: Mark for everyone!

SPCK
ISBN: 0-2810-5299-9

Price: £8.99

£6.99 with voucher

First published in 2001 by SPCK
Holy Trinity Church, Marylebone Road,
London, NW1 4DU

MARK 14.12–25

The Last Supper

[12]On the first day of unleavened bread, when the Passover lambs were sacrificed, Jesus' disciples said to him,

'Where would you like us to go and get things ready for you to eat the Passover?'

[13]He sent off two of his disciples, with these instructions.

'Go into the city, and you will be met by a man carrying a water-pot. Follow him. [14]When he goes indoors, say to the master of the house, "The teacher says, where is the guest room for me, where I can eat the Passover with my disciples?" [15]He will show you a large upstairs room, set out and ready. Make preparations for us there.'

[16]The disciples went out, entered the city, and found it exactly as he had said. They prepared the Passover.

[17]When it was evening, Jesus came with the Twelve. [18]As they were reclining at table and eating, Jesus said, 'I'm telling you the truth: one of you is going to betray me – one of you that's eating with me.'

[19]They began to be very upset, and to say to one another,

'It isn't me, is it?'

[20]'It's one of the Twelve,' said Jesus, 'one who has dipped his bread in the dish with me. [21]Yes: the son of man is completing his journey, as scripture said he would; but it's bad news for the man who betrays him! It would have been better for that man never to have been born.'

[22]While they were eating, he took bread, blessed it, broke it, and gave it to them.

'Take it,' he said. 'This is my body.'

[23]Then he took the cup, gave thanks, and gave it to them, and they all drank from it.

[24]'This is my blood of the covenant,' he said, 'which is poured out for many. [25]I'm telling you the truth: I won't ever drink from the fruit of the vine again, until that day – the day when I drink it new in the kingdom of God.'

On my fortieth birthday, my students gave me a surprise party. While I was taking a service in the college chapel, they carefully cleared the papers in my room, decorated it from floor to ceiling, and laid out a magnificent spread, with cakes and wine at the middle of it. I knew nothing about it until I walked through the door. It was a marvellous and memorable evening.

It's a deep human instinct – I believe a God-given one – that we mark significant moments with significant meals. Sharing a meal, especially a festive one, binds together a family, a group of friends, a collection of colleagues. Such meals say more than we could ever put into words about who we are, how we feel about one another, and the hopes and joys that we share together. The meal not only feeds our bodies; that seems in some ways the least significant part of it. It *says* something; and it *does* something, actually changing us so that, after it, part of who we actually are is 'the people who shared that meal together, with all that it meant'.

The great Jewish festivals all function in this way, most of them connected to the retelling of some part of the story of how God has rescued Israel from slavery in Egypt. Supreme among the festivals was Passover, when they not only told the story of how God had liberated them, but used to recline on couches at the table; in that world, free people didn't just sit, they reclined. Celebrating Passover was and is a deeply religious act, and also, for the many centuries in which Jews have suffered oppression, a deeply political act. It says, loud and clear, 'despite appearances, we are God's free people? It sustains loyalty; it encourages **faith**, hope and love.

Take all that for granted, and now come into Jerusalem with the unsuspecting **disciples** as they follow one of Jesus' unnamed, secret friends in the city to an unidentified location. Jesus knows the end can't be far off, but he is determined that this Passover meal will be uninterrupted. This meal will say what he most wants to say to his followers, and because it's to be repeated, it will go on saying it. This meal will do what needs to be done, again and again, changing his followers, making them the people who depend on his death for their life, the people who discover that through his achievement God's **kingdom** is now coming on earth as in **heaven**. In that sense, the meal is a surprise party for the disciples, though it turns out to be a very sad one.

All the two know is that they're getting ready the special elements that make up the traditional Jewish Passover. What Jesus knows is that this will be a Passover with a difference. This is the time when he will go, as a greater Moses, ahead of the **Twelve**, ahead of Israel, ahead of the world, into the presence of a greater slave-master than Pharaoh, into a terror greater than walking through the sea, to lead the world to freedom. This Passover-meal-with-a-difference is going to *explain*, more deeply than words could ever do, what his action, and passion, the next day really meant; and, more than explaining it, it will enable Jesus' followers, from that day to this, to make it their own, to draw life and strength from it. If we want to understand, and be nourished by, what happened on Calvary, this meal is the place to start.

Jesus has, for some time now, been trying to teach the disciples about his forthcoming death; they have been, to put it mildly, slow to catch on. He has given a few words of explanation and interpretation, in terms of biblical background (the **son of man**, the servant), political meaning (turning worldly notions of rulership on their heads), and theological interpretation (giving his life a ransom for many). All of that lies behind this meal, but the meal itself goes far beyond theory.

To the annoyance of our rationalistic age, you can't put this meaning into words. You can only put it into action. Actions like this are so powerful that sometimes people in the churches have tried to contain or control them, to surround them with more and more words, like trying to cage in a tiger. But the actions – taking, blessing, breaking and giving the bread; taking, blessing and giving the cup – cannot be caged.

Of course, some words are necessary, otherwise the actions would degenerate into magic, perhaps unconnected with Jesus, with the historical moment of his death. The words Jesus himself used are crucial to the event. Jesus, we must assume, told the Passover story, as the head of the family always would; but this time, instead of saying words to link the bread and the wine back to the **Exodus** and forward to the final liberation of Israel, he said new words, which linked them directly to the death he would very shortly die, and to the coming of the kingdom of God that would be brought about by that death. This meal, with all its new-passover associations, was Jesus' primary means of enabling his followers not only to understand his death but to let it do its freedom-work in their lives and in the world. It drew to a head the kingdom-actions (not least the feast-ings) and kingdom-teaching of his whole public career. Jesus' death, seen and known in the light of this meal, makes sense of it all. This is how the kingdom will come.

All the more tragic, then, that on that night Jesus also spoke sorrowful words about someone who would betray him. They had come in secret to a secret destination; it would take treachery from within to put Jesus at the authori-ties' mercy. Jesus, with the scriptures in his head (not least passages in the Psalms which spoke of betrayal by an intimate friend), knew it was bound to happen, but grieved for the torment that would be suffered by the traitor.

Since this meal was and is so central, we shouldn't be surprised that its meaning, and the way it is enacted, has often been the subject of bitter disputes and divisions within the church. Sorrow hung over the Last Supper itself, and sorrow hangs over every re-enactment of it within a divided church. But the meal itself, whether kept simply or magnificently, whether the words are whispered or sung, towers above the disputes and failures of Jesus' followers then and now. Jesus intended it to be the central means whereby his kingdom-achieving death would be known, believed, appropriated and lived out. Each generation of Christians, and each subculture within Christianity, must find ways of enabling that to happen.

MARK 14.26–52

Jesus Is Arrested

[26]They sang a hymn, and went out to the Mount of Olives.

[27]'You're all going to desert me,' said Jesus, 'because it's written,

"I shall attack the shepherd

And then the sheep will scatter."

[28]'But after I am raised up, I will go ahead of you to Galilee.'

[29]Peter spoke up.

'Everyone else may desert you,' he said, 'but I won't.'

[30]'I'm telling you the truth,' Jesus replied. 'Today – this very night, before the cock has crowed twice – you will renounce me three times.'

[31]This made Peter all the more vehement.

'Even if I have to die with you he said, 'I will never renounce you.'

And all the rest said the same.

[32]They came to a place called Gethsemane.

'Stay here', said Jesus to the disciples, 'while I pray.'

[33]He took Peter, James and John with him, and became quite overcome and deeply distressed.

[34] "My soul is disturbed within me", he said, 'right to the point of death. Stay here and keep watch.'

[35] He went a little further, and fell on the ground and prayed that, if possible, the moment might pass from him.

[36] 'Abba, Father,' he said, 'all things are possible for you! Take this cup away from me! But – not what I want, but what you want.'

[37] He returned and found them sleeping.

'Are you asleep, Simon?' he said to Peter. 'Couldn't you keep watch for a single hour? [38] Watch and pray, so that you won't come into the time of trouble. The spirit is eager, but the body is weak.'

[39] Once more he went off and prayed, saying the same words. [40] And again, when he returned, he found them asleep, because their eyes were very heavy. They had no words to answer him. [41] But the third time he came, he said to them,

'All right – sleep as much as you like now. Have a good rest. The job is done, the time has come – and look! The son of man is betrayed into the clutches of sinners. [42] Get up, let's be on our way. Here comes the man who's going to betray me.'

At once, while he was still speaking, Judas, one of the Twelve, arrived, accompanied by a crowd, with swords and clubs, from the chief priests, the lawyers, and the elders. The betrayer had given them a coded sign: 'The one I kiss – that's him! Seize him and take him away safely.'

[45] He came up to Jesus at once. 'Rabbi!' he said, and kissed him.

[46] The crowd laid hands on him and seized him. [47] One of the bystanders drew a sword and struck the high priest's servant, cutting off his ear. [48] Then Jesus spoke to them.

'Anyone would think', he said, 'you'd come after a brigand! Fancy needing swords and clubs to arrest me! [49]Day after day I've been teaching in the Temple, under your noses, and you never laid a finger on me. But the scriptures must be fulfilled.'

[50]Then they all abandoned him and ran away.

[51]A young man had followed him, wearing only a linen tunic over his otherwise naked body. [52]They seized him, and he left the tunic and ran away naked.

What do you do when the strong person in your life suddenly becomes weak?

Children face this when the parent on whom they have relied for everything is suddenly struck down with illness or grief. Colleagues working on a project are thrown into confusion if the team leader suddenly loses confidence. A church is dismayed if the pastor or preacher suddenly loses **faith**, or hope, or integrity.

We can only begin to imagine the effect on the **disciples** of the sudden change that came over Jesus in Gethsemane. Until that moment he had been in control: planning, directing, teaching, guiding. He had always been ready with a word or action. Now he is, as we say, falling apart, and warning them that they are going to collapse around him. As well they might.

The scene is so intimate and frightening that we feel almost embarrassed to be onlookers. Jesus' own horror, and the disciples' sleepy dismay, are raw human emotion, naked and unadorned. When the great Greek philosopher Socrates went to his death, he was calm and in control throughout the process. His followers, though distraught and in tears, remembered his steady teaching right up to the end, his coolly ironic last words. Not so with Jesus. This story is neither a Greek-style heroic tale nor a typical Jewish martyrdom. It is unique. Only if we enter into it – which we can hardly do without fear and trembling on our own part – will we understand the human depths, and hence the theological depths, of the story.

Once again we have a central scene flanked by two outer ones. In the middle is Jesus in the garden, overcome with horror, praying for another way, claiming the truth he had already taught the disciples (10.27), that all things are possible to God – and being told that there was no turning back. As ever, the Psalms give him words to express his torment, this time in a quotation from the refrain of Psalms 42 and 43 (42.5, 11; 43.5; 'Why so heavy, my soul? Why so disturbed within me?'). He comes through a time of great struggle, a three-times repeated prayer for rescue; eventually, it seems, he hears from the one he calls 'Abba, Father' the answer: No. ('Abba' is the Aramaic word for 'father'; not simply a children's word, but always carrying intimate affection and devotion.) If even Jesus received that answer to one of his most heartfelt prayers, we should not be surprised if sometimes it's that way for us too. He emerges, composed and in charge once more, though his last words to the disciples are full of ironic contradiction: 'Carry on sleeping – get up and let's go!'

To one side of this central scene is Jesus' frightening conversation with the disciples. They will all, he says, abandon him. Again he is conscious of scriptural warnings, all of which he senses rushing together into a dense fulfilment. He has shepherded his little flock, from the time he gathered them in Galilee until now; now he, the shepherd, will be struck down, and for a time at least the flock will run away to wherever they can hide. Even this, though it will reflect their cowardice and confusion, is part of the plan: Jesus must go alone into the 'time of trouble', the great dark moment that is coming upon him. The disciples have no place there. They must pray to be spared it.

And Peter, the Rock – impetuous as ever, opening his mouth first and thinking afterwards – Peter will be turned inside out by the whole process. The triple prayer of Jesus in the garden will find a ghastly parody in the triple renunciation that Peter will make. Three times Jesus will place himself in the hands, and the will, of his Abba. Three times Peter, Jesus' right-hand man, will deny that he even knows him.

To the other side of the central scene is Jesus' betrayal and arrest. Judas has found the perfect place: in the dark, outside the city, away from the crowds. The swords and clubs are unnecessary; they imply that Jesus is the kind of revolutionary leader that he has steadfastly refused to be, despite what many had hoped. Indeed, Judas himself may have wanted that kind of **Messiah**; the irony increases with every step.

One of the disciples gets carried away and tries to fight. John identifies him as Peter, but the others leave him anonymous, and Mark, aware of how out of keeping this behaviour was, won't even identify him as one of Jesus' followers, but just says 'one of the bystanders'. In the same way, though Mark has been talking in verses 48–49 about the crowd who have come to arrest Jesus, when in verse 50 he describes the disciples running away, he doesn't call them 'disciples'. He just says 'they all abandoned him and ran away'. They are not behaving as disciples, so he refuses them the title.

Finally, we have the young man who, like Joseph in Genesis 39.12, escapes by leaving his garment behind. It's often been suggested that this was Mark himself (the other **gospels** don't mention the incident); though it's impossible to prove it, it is a quite reasonable guess. Whether or not that is so, the imagery is striking, going back as far as Genesis 3. Like Adam and Eve, the disciples are metaphorically, and in this case literally, hiding their naked shame in the garden. Their disgrace is complete.

Gethsemane invites us to consider, above all, what it meant for Jesus to be, in a unique sense, God's son. The very moment of greatest intimacy – the desperate prayer to 'Abba, Father' – is also the moment where, hearing the answer 'No', he is set on the course for the moment of God-forsakenness on the cross (15.34). Until we have come to terms with this, we have not really begun to think what we mean when we say the Christian creeds.

The triple scene invites us to stop and ponder, once more, where we ourselves belong. Are we, like the disciples, full of bluster one minute, sleep the next, and confused shame the next? Are we ready to betray Jesus if it suits our other plans, or if he fails to live up to our expectations? Or are we prepared to keep watch with him in the garden, sharing his anguished prayer? We are not called to repeat his unique moment of suffering; he went through that alone on behalf of us all. But as Christian writers from the very beginning (i.e. Paul) have seen, it is part of normal Christian experience that we, too, should be prepared to agonize in prayer as we await our own complete redemption and that of all creation. The church is called to live in the middle of this great scene: surrounded by confusion, false loyalty, direct attack and traitor's kisses, those who name the name of Christ must stay in the garden with him until the Father's will is done.

Thank God It's Monday

Mark Greene

This fun, fast and full-of-stories book takes a practical look at how we can make the most of our time at work.

It examines our jobs, colleagues and bosses from God's point of view and helps us realise that God is at work there through us, in us, and in those we work with. The third edition of this highly influential contemporary classic features an updated resource section and a new chapter on integrating life and work, helping us to see how our work life, as well as our weekend life, can be lived fruitfully for God.

Scripture Union
ISBN: 1-8599-9503-9

Price: £5.99

£3.99 with voucher

First published in 2001 by Scripture Union
207-209 Queensway, Bletchley, Milton Keynes, MK2 2EB

Chapter 7

GETTING A LIFE

or The power of 'No'

'Do trawler fishermen love their children?'
'Yes,' she replied, 'at a distance.'

Monique Potter

About twenty years ago Brian started working in a bank.
He got in at nine, left at five and had a lunch hour. Today he
is still working for the same bank. But he gets in at eight,
leaves at six-thirty, and lunch, well, lunch in the old sense of
the word – sitting across a table from a human being and
having a meal – lunch is for wimps. Lunch today is sitting
across a desk from a warm PC, snatching sporadic bites out
of a sandwich.

Brian doesn't work long hours because he is cosmically
ambitious. He doesn't work long hours because he wants a
holiday in St Tropez, a Ferrari in the garage or an Armani
suit in his wardrobe. He works long hours because long
hours are what you do if you want to stay in work. Because,
so the popular wisdom goes, if you don't they'll find
someone else who will.

The dynamics of contemporary work

British workers work longer hours than any other nation in the EU. They are suffering increasing levels of stress, anxiety and depression, with less relational satisfaction, less sense of purpose and significance, and, consequently, with greater pressure on every other area of their lives. The Institute of Management Report showed that 'concern about the lack of balance in respondents' lives and the negative effects of long hours, both personally and in terms of their productivity, has increased dramatically' And as you can see from the chart below, it's getting worse:

Impact of long hours

	1997 %	1999 %
No time for other interests:	77	87
Damaging health:	59	71
Affects relationship negatively with children:	73	86
with partner:	72	79
Reduces productivity over time:	55	68

Source: *The Quality of Working Life, 1999, Survey of Managers' Changing Experiences,* Les Worrall & Cary Cooper, Institute of Management.

People may want their boss's job but they don't want their boss's life. This is not just a middle-class, white-collar phenomenon – workers at every level are suffering. This is a *slave* new world.

And if work doesn't work, life tends not to work either. This is a great source of pain, anguish, depression and conflict for many individuals and families. Indeed, increasingly it seems that the requirements for success, or even survival at work, are diametrically opposed to the requirements of good marriages and good parenthood. Long hours and long marriages are often not compatible.

The dynamics of contemporary life

The pressure that many people feel at work is aggravated by the increasingly impersonal dynamics of life in Britain. Almost everything about twenty-first century life tends to reduce the number of significant relationships we have.

We shop in impersonal malls rather than in towns where we might meet people we know. Most of us don't know the names of our neighbours, and our towns are becoming dormitories not communities. We travel further to work, to school, to university We live further away from our relatives and the friends we grew up with. And so on and on and on, as the ad goes. Virtually everything about contemporary life tends to diminish people's sense that they have a place in the world independent of their work.

So, can we get a life? And what does that mean anyway?

In your view, which (if any) of the following people do you think has a life?

Larry is one of the leading lawyers in his field in the country He leaves his house at about six-thirty every day, and he usually gets back by eight-thirty. He has a wife and three teenage children. He often leads worship in his home church. He preaches from time to time, administers a Trust and is involved in a variety of Christian ministries.

Does he have a life?

Holly is a 35-year-old housewife with three children aged 2, 5 and 7. She works at home, gets up at six forty-five, prepares the kids for school, cleans the house, does five loads of washing a week, does the shopping, prepares food, helps with homework, goes to a ladies' Bible Study one morning a week, has the occasional coffee with a friend, and spends at least five hours a day without adult company.

Does she have a life?

Interestingly, in seminars, most people felt that Larry the Lawyer didn't have a life and that Holly the housewife did. But in fact, the real Larry felt that he *did* have a life and the real Holly didn't. This may be because we impose cultural expectations on people which are precisely that and no more. Larry's children don't feel he has a life, not because they don't have a good relationship with him they do – but because he works so hard that they don't see him doing what they might call 'fun' things. But Larry enjoys many of the things he does and believes he is fulfilling his duties before God. One man's fun is another man's drudgery

Holly doesn't feel that she has a life because, although her life is in many ways privileged, she doesn't get to do the things she does best and from which she gains most refreshment.

After all, not all women who choose to stay at home do so because they find the work exhilarating! Many believe that God wants them there to look after the children when they're young. This may look idyllic from the outside, but it is often crushingly lonely and debilitating. A mother may love her children but not find any real refreshment for her soul doing five loads of washing a week – separating the whites and the coloureds, loading the machine, hanging up the wet washing, taking down the dry washing, ironing the washing and putting it into drawers.

Some church cultures value this role extremely highly and use such language as 'the biblical woman.' In truth, such terminology is deeply misleading – the picture of the woman working in and close to the home primarily reflects the lifestyle of pre-industrial societies and does not necessarily provide a theological blueprint for mother-hood in the information age.

That said, there is an enormous 'care deficit' in our society – and the best thing is not always the most enjoy-able for our selves in the short term, nor the most affirmed. Unlike much work outside the home, many homemakers have no performance appraisal or end-of-year bonus, or even a decent helping of basic appreciation or encouragement.

Again, it is dangerous to impose one particular view of the 'good life' on everyone.

The danger of balance?

Much Christian writing on the problem of work and life focuses on the word 'balance.' We are exhorted to get a proper 'balance' between time with God, time with family, time at work, time in leisure, and so on. The problem with this approach is that it is simply not biblical. It is not clear at all that Jesus or Paul led 'balanced' lives, in the sense that contemporary writers mean it.

Furthermore, this notion of balance often seems to present us with a 1950s view of American family life. Where does it say in the Bible, as one young wife put it, that husbands have to be home at six o'clock? Where does it say that a person cannot work sixty hours a week and still be in the centre of God's will? Where does it say that I have to pursue a hobby to be refreshed? Maybe my job refreshes me? And often mine does.

In the Bible we don't get a life – we get 'life', abundant life. In the Bible the call is not to 'balance' but to obedience. And the question of what Christ requires of each of us is central. This inevitably varies. My former boss, Peter Cotterell, was once asked how many hours people should work in a week? 'That depends,' he replied, 'on their capacity and their life-stage.' Some people are capable of sixty hours' intense, focused work without burning themselves out – but most are not. Some people can choose to work longer hours because their other responsibilities allow them to do so.

So, a parent with young children may well want to maximise the time they spend with their children. But a woman whose children have left home may well want to work sixty hours a week because she enjoys it or because she believes that this is her duty before God.

The Bible doesn't tell us how many hours to work, but it does give us clear indicators of what the healthy life looks like in general – that is, it does set down certain priorities. After we've examined those priorities, we'll look at some guidelines for possible change.

Biblical priorities

• We are commanded to develop an intimate relationship with God (Deut 6:5).

Does my overall life allow me to do this? If not, is it because of my work pattern or the way I use my leisure time? Is it because I fail to see what God is teaching me in my workplace, or is it because I feel that I have no time to devote to prayer and to listening to God through his word?

Or is it simply because I am ill-disciplined?

• We are commanded to love others (Matt 22:39).

Christians are meant to be in relationships. We have obligations to our parents, our spouses, our children, our friends and to the household of God.

Now the Bible does not tell us how much time to spend with our children, but it does tell us, for example, that parents – fathers *and* mothers – are to teach their children about God (Deut 4:9–10). This is not something that can be 'outsourced' to a youthworker or to a Sunday school teacher. And you can't teach children without spending time with them, nor can you give them a deep sense of security and love if you are never there, or only there in an exhausted and depleted state. Sometimes this creates tough choices.

Derek was doing well in a London property company. He was offered a partnership. But he turned it down because it would mean he would have to sign a contract that would require him regularly to work later than five-thirty, and that would mean a savage encroachment on his time with his family. In fact, he was offered a partnership eleven years in a row. He turned it down each time. Financially, this was probably the difference between a Ferrari and a Fiesta, but a Fiesta still gets you to work, and probably more reliably.

In the twelfth year, the company offered him a partnership without requiring him to work regularly beyond five-thirty. Derek had the confidence to set aside the extra financial reward, the status of being a partner, and so on, for the sake of a higher priority – his relationship with his family. He chose time over money.

This is self-evidently easier if you are already in a well-paid job, but not everyone is in that situation. Anyway, we are not all 'Dereks', not all as good at our jobs as he is. The choice is not always between 'enough' and 'more', but rather between 'more' and 'nothing'. However, many people, particularly people in so-called white-collar jobs, have a range of skills that are more transferable than they realise.

That said, Derek's choice was Derek's choice before God. This does not necessarily mean that the person who works sixty hours a week and commutes a further ten hours is out of God's will. In fact, the person who works sixty hours a week and commutes ten may well have very good relationships with their family. Certainly, this is the case with one or two senior executives I know. Their ability to focus on their families when they are with them, to create opportunities to build intimacy and contribute significantly to church life, belies traditional guilt-inducing analyses of how the Christian life should be led.

But such people are rare. Many, many families have been sacrificed on the altar of a workaholic's addiction, whether that workaholic is a business person or, for that matter, a pastor or missionary Some pressures are self-imposed and the result of misdirected ambition or covetousness.

The Bible not only tells us that the quality of our relationships with God and others is vital, it also tells us that:

• We are commanded to work (Exod 20:9).

We are *meant* to work. But we work for a purpose, and part of that purpose is to provide for ourselves and for other people for whom we have responsibilities. We are not commanded to work in such a way that it results in the relational and spiritual neglect of those we are called to care for.

- We are commanded to stop working (Exod 20:10). We are called on to rest and to seek refreshment.

Here again, we need to recognise that one person's refreshment is another person's agony. This fact relates to how God has made us as individuals. We are often refreshed when we do something that we do best, that we have been created to do. Some people gain curious satisfaction from cooking, or dancing, or from making a set of numbers add up – or from selling a car!

The question for many people is about whether their over all life gives them opportunities to flourish as human beings. This involves both fulfilling duties and having the opportunity to be a good steward of what God has entrusted to us – people, gifts and resources.

A helpful exercise

The following is an exercise that will help you to identify your HFQ – your **Human Flourishing Quotient**.

Score yourself on a scale of 1 to 10 (10 is 'yes' and great; 1 is 'no' and awful).

My relationship with God is flourishing, and I get about the right amount of time with him.
I get about the right amount of time for family/key relationships.

I get about the right amount of sleep.
I get about the right amount of time for rest.
I get to do things that refresh me reasonably often.
My lifestyle allows me to stay reasonably healthy.
I get about the right amount of time for church life.
I work about the right amount of time.
I'm reasonably satisfied with the structure of my life.
I feel that there's another Christian who knows me, to whom I can open up my life.

Total ....

How did you do?

Obviously, the HFQ is a blunt instrument and some aspects of our lives are more important than others, but anything over 70 would be very good; 50–69 and there's certainly room for improvement; under 50 and, well, you're probably very keen to find a way to make some changes. Is there a way forward?

Change for the better

Well, supposing your HFQ scored less than 50, what could you do to change the situation? Here are a few suggestions:

• Realign your priorities with God's priorities and your responsibilities.

Does your life reflect your priorities? Does it reflect your desire to know God better and to serve him in all you do? Or not? What would the people who know you well say?

Here there is need for care. Some people may not be entirely objective: a work colleague who knows you well might say you don't work as hard as anyone else in the office. Your pastor might say you're working too hard because you're not available to lead a home group, clean the church, attend prayer meetings. But is that what God requires – or, rather, what an old model of service in the local church used to require? Is that model realistic or even helpful today?

What would happen if you blocked out a clear twenty minutes a day to spend with God? What would happen if you decided to get all the household chores done before Sunday?

Similarly, many married men – and this does seem to apply to men more than women – feel that however much time they spend at home it wouldn't be enough for their spouses. Talking this through is vital. What does the job actually require? If it's too much, what can be done? Are those choices acceptable – for example, making do with less money, a smaller house?

What would happen if you took your work calendar and blocked out, a year ahead, all significant birthdays, anniversaries a year, school engagements, church away-weekends, etc? What would happen if you took your calendar and blocked out one evening a week when you leave work at the 'official' leaving time and informed those you worked with that you would normally be leaving at that time on that day?

And who is the right person to whom you can remain accountable?

• Change your attitude to the life you have.

Are you simply failing to count your blessings? Failing to recognise that your relationship with God could be vibrant and intimate if only you saw that he was at work with you, if only you saw your work as a context where he does in fact teach you, speak to you, use you and shape you?

Are you harbouring anger? Two of the primary causes of stress are unresolved anger and feeling powerless to change one's circumstances. Many, many people are angry with the situation they find themselves in: angry with their companies, angry with themselves for not being able to change their situation, angry about the choices they have made in the past. And this anger can lead to depression and contribute to the general sense of weariness that pervades the workplace, as a recent survey of 20,000 people revealed. The survey was sponsored by a nutrition company, so it's not surprising that their solutions were primarily dietary. This situation, however, will not be resolved by cutting down on caffeine, upping your fruit and vegetable intake, and eating raw nuts and seeds. Nor is this pandemic of exhaustion and stress to be cured by applying *Little Book of Calm* inanities ('picture yourself on an idyllic South Pacific Island'), or using worry beads, or yes, you guessed it – changing your diet (more wheatgerm and lentils).

Clearly, if anger is a cause of your stress, that needs to be dealt with – through learning to forgive others, to forgive yourself, and so on. However, we also need to ask ourselves if there are some aspects of our behaviour we could change.

• Change aspects of your behaviour.

It may be true that you don't have any spare time, but it may also be true that what you do with your limited time does not contribute well to your overall flourishing. We say that we have no time, but we watch twenty hours of TV a week. We have no time to read our Bibles, but we read the paper for forty minutes on the journey into work. We feel that we just can't get away from work, but we don't turn off our mobiles and we check the home PC for work messages within seconds of walking through the front door.

It may be true that you don't have enough time, but is it that you are simply over-ambitious, or ambitious for the wrong reasons? Ambitious because you gain your sense of identity and self-worth from your work? Ambitious because you have something to prove to yourself? Because you want the very best for your family, but forget perhaps that your family might prefer to stand by the sink doing the dishes with you than listen to the low hum of the sleek Bosch dishwasher while your dinner slumps forlornly on a plate in the microwave.

Perhaps you spend more time at work because that is where you get your affirmation. Work becomes your 'idol' because, through work and at work, people tell you that you're won derful – while at home things may be more complex, more difficult. There is plenty of anecdotal evidence that some husbands deliberately work late to avoid the strain of putting several young children to bed – getting them cleaned, toileted, brushed, read to and prayed for without World War 3 breaking out. Easier to tell a client you're going to be two weeks late on their project …

The question of how behaviour contributes to long hours also applies at work. Over 30 per cent of people who use computers admit to spending more than two hours a day 'skiving' – not doing the work assigned by the company but simply playing on the machine. I'm home late but I've reached level 97 in Kill-the-Boss II. Are there ways to work a little bit more efficiently? The danger is that we may become less focused precisely because we have got used to working long hours. We're doing a ten-hour day, so what's the problem with a ten-minute chat by the photocopier?

Here too we need to manage other people's expectations of us. If the boss says he needs it tomorrow, does he? If everyone works till seven, do they need to? And do you? In one national survey, 68 per cent of people felt pressured to work longer than their colleagues. If we all bow to that pressure, there will be no end to work.

- Change the terms of your job.

A number of people have changed the terms of their employment, shifting to a four-day week, or electing to work at home one or two days a week and thereby reducing the wear and tear of travel. Famously, Nicola Horlick, a high-level financial executive, asked her senior management if she could shift to working four days. Initially, they refused because they believed that if they allowed her to do that, then all the men would want the same. She told her management they wouldn't. And she was right – they didn't. But some of them could have.

It's clear that in some jobs – high finance, commercial law, and so on – very long hours are required when deals are being made. But is it also a requirement for executives to move from one job to the next without a break? Are there ways to build in time off in lieu into work practice? Yes, but only if employees are prepared to accept less money.

• Change corporate ethos and structures.

This sounds idealistic, but it may not be. Some companies don't set out to create working practices that are inimical to life – it just turns out that way. Meetings are called at times that make it impossible to get home for supper. This may simply happen because the boss lives a mile away from the office and hasn't considered others or because many of the staff are single and so not all that aware of a married person's situation. Again, voicing concern or saying 'No' may be enough to change the culture.

At a macro level, much of the increased pressure on workers relates to the need to improve quarterly earnings in order to sustain shareholder value. The question is: could this be achieved in another way? Can business leaders make work more humane and therefore more sustainable, and equally profitable. If work is more humane, it is easier (and cheaper) to attract and retain talented people. And talented people may well give the company the distinctive competitive edge it requires in a highly competitive environment.

Furthermore, more humane working practice means that absenteeism goes down, and the workforce is happier. And that, research indicates, tends to lead to happier customers, which in turn leads to higher profitability. Could it be done?

• Change job.

Why not? Because this is the job you feel God has called you to? Good reason. Because you don't believe you can get another one? That may be a good reason, if it were in fact true. But it is not true for most people under 45. Many people have more transferable skills than they realise.

Perhaps you should think about signing up for one of those one-day courses that help you see how your experience and current skill-base might be used elsewhere, or what new skills you could acquire. You may not find a new job, but knowing you might be able to may help enormously with coping with the present one.

Still, the question remains: even if you changed your job to one that was less demanding of your time, would your relationship with God and others be significantly improved, or not? Maybe, in an over-busy world, it's easy to blame work.

The reality is that the way we work is corroding British life. As such, cracking this problem is not just vital for Christians, it is vital for our non-Christian colleagues. It is, potentially, an enormously powerful witness to them. If we carry on accepting the system as it is, we consign ourselves and our society to ever-deepening misery But if we can find ways to work and live well, we will not only enjoy life but be the agents of liberation that we are called to be.

This, of course, is no small task. No serious commentator, secular or otherwise, doubts that Britain is in the grip of a form of Anglo-American capitalism that has succeeded in breaking down almost all constraints on working hours which do not relate to issues of physical safety. The statutory 48-hour limit carries little weight in reality

To change this world represents an enormous challenge, particularly when church employment culture is, in many respects, more demanding – long hours, crushing levels of stress, poorer support mechanisms, lower pay. In reality, while we may bemoan current working practices 'in the world', we allow or often expect our pastors to work under greater stress, with poorer resources, and virtually no meaningful budget for in-service training. If we want to change the system, we will simply have to make a stand and say 'No' – creatively and diplomatically, perhaps, but firmly – and be prepared to accept the consequences. As Derek did when he refused that partnership for eleven years.

Snapshot

A while back, I found myself in the front seat of a Mondeo mini-cab with a driver who only works for business accounts. He told me that he had had the opportunity to upgrade to a Mercedes which would have enabled him to command higher fares. 'But', he said, 'I make what I need.' And it was enough.

Enough.

Now there's a novel concept.

Living on Purpose

Tom and Christine Sine

Whether it is our career, or rushing children to a football match or dancing class, we settle for less and miss God's best for our life. We live in Boom City while pretending we embrace the values of the City of Shalom.

The aim of this book is to help us find the enormous satisfaction of living on purpose. Tom and Christine outline imaginative ways to reinvent our lifestyles and timetables, to reflect the purposes and rhythms of God's Kingdom. Discover a more festive, less stressed way of living. It could just save your life.

Monarch
ISBN:1-8542.4520-1

Price:£7.99

£5.99 with voucher

First published in 2002 by Monarch Books
Broadway House, The Broadway, Crowborough,
East Sussex, TN6 1HQ

Looking for God's Best in All the Wrong Places

The clock is my dictator, I shall not rest.
It makes me lie down only when exhausted
It leads me to deep depression, it hounds my soul.
It leads me in circles of frenzy for activity's sake.
Even though I run frantically from task to task,
I will never get it all done, for my "ideal" is with me.
Deadlines and my need for approval, they drive me.
They demand performance from me, beyond the
  limits of my schedule.
They anoint my head with migraines, my in-basket
  overflows.
Surely fatigue and time pressure shall follow me all
  the days of my life,
And I will dwell in the bonds of frustration forever.

Marcia K. Hornok, *Psalm 23, Antithesis*[1]

Going for the gold

Going for the Gold, Extreme Cool, High Status, I Want to be a Millionaire, A Mo Betta Life Man! Everyone is going for the gold. We are all racing along the freeway of life in our quest for the best. Where are we likely to find the good life for ourselves and those we care about? If the skyline of that land of milk and honey suddenly appeared over the next horizon would we even recognize it? Or could we be taken in by some very seductive, glittering counterfeits and take the wrong exit?

Finding the focus

We are convinced that deep down inside everyone wants the best God has for them. People are looking for the good life, which at its core includes wanting a satisfying way of life that counts for something. But the evidence suggests that most of us are missing the best and settling for less … often a lot less. We are surrounded by many stories and competing visions of what constitutes the best … the good life and better future. The most prevalent story that fills our world today is a product of modern culture and our new global economy. The dream of the good life and better future at the centre of this story is a dream of economic growth, individual upscaling and ever expanding consumer choice that we call Boom City. And its dazzling skyline has become the most attractive dream for people all over the planet.

In this chapter we will argue that if we don't draft a mission statement that flows directly out of our faith, like Jesus did, then Boom City will define our mission statement for us. While many of us are constantly aware that the pressures we are under make our lives one long stress-race, we don't seem to understand where the pressure comes from. We seem to be largely unaware that many of us, including very sincere Christians, have allowed Boom City instead of our faith to define what's best for our lives and families. To the extent that we allow the dream that drives Boom City to define the direction and tempo for our lives and families; to that extent you can be sure we will miss the best that God has for us.

One reason numbers of us are beginning to question whether we are headed in the right direction is that we find ourselves trapped in the fast lane literally burning the rubber right off our tyres. A new contagion called "hurry sickness" is sweeping across the world. Hurry sickness is simply the consequence of people trying to jam more activity into 24 hours than is humanly possible … and becoming hyper-stressed in the process. Everywhere we work in Britain, Australia, New Zealand, Canada and the US, most people tell us they have to work harder and longer in this new global economy than even a few years ago.

As John Ortberg expressed in *The Life You've Always Wanted*, "One of the great delusions of our day is that hurrying will buy us more time."[2] Ortberg goes on to say "If we have hurry sickness, we are haunted by the fear that there are just not enough hours in the day to do what needs to be done. We will read faster, walk faster, talk faster, and when listening, nod faster to encourage the talker to accelerate. We will find our selves chafing whenever we have to wait."[3] Hurry sickness is an epidemic sweeping across our world. It stresses our lives and leaves us exhausted and chronically guilty for all that we haven't done. Can you find some of your symptoms in this quick review of the afflicted?

Juggling with Julie in an on-line life

Julie is a 42-year-old mum who sees herself as a totally incompetent circus juggler. When she is home, her cell phone and beeper constantly interrupt meals and limit her family time. Each morning she staggers out of bed at 5 am in her London home so she can check her 65 e-mails before waking her two kids. She dashes out the door before they are off to school and races to the train. Her beeper goes off … reminding her that she should be home to take her oldest daughter to have braces fitted at 4 pm that day. But she won't be home until evening, so she grabs her cell phone to call her husband. Perhaps he can leave work early. But her cell phone is dead and she realizes she won't be able to call him until after he finishes with clients for the day. Julie sinks into her chair exhausted, feeling guilty because she has just dropped the ball yet again.

One reason people like Julie are so busy is that in the nineties the workplace changed dramatically. Now that we are all part of a new global economy, a growing number of us never leave work. In this new "hyperconnected" world many of us are on-line and on call 24 hours a day, 7 days a week, creating what has become known as a 24/7 lifestyle. Life has become a kind of extreme sport for many. The *New York Times* heralds, "Cell phones, pagers and wireless e-mail have created a workday that never ends. Whatever line people have drawn between work and leisure, between office and home is growing thinner than ever as a sense of obligation to stay connected to work all hours continues to grow."[4]

Sleepless in Cambridge with Matthew

Matthew is a 22-year-old student in a rush. He is in his final year at Cambridge and is anxious to complete his business degree so that he can start earning a six-figure income instead of "giving his money away" to the university. Matt seldom misses a lecture but is trying to restrict himself to four hours sleep a night so that he can run his small web-page business from 4 to 8 am before going to his 9 am class. He seems to be doing a better job than Julie of keeping all his balls in the air — except for one thing. In the last six months he has suffered increasingly from blackouts. He didn't worry when he occasionally blacked out in the library or even in class. But when he rolled his car on his way to Edinburgh last week it got his attention and he made an appointment for a checkup at the health clinic.

For Matthew and millions of other Westerners, stress, exhaustion and extreme busyness have become badges of distinction. "The frenetic sense of lost time and life out of control permeates our entire modern society."[5] Less than 67 per cent of adults in the US get 8 hours sleep. Some 43 per cent are so sleepy during the day that, like Matthew, they have serious problems functioning. Research reveals that we are getting a lot less sleep than we used to. Fifty-eight per cent of people surveyed said they suffered from insomnia at least a couple of nights a week, while 45 per cent said they would willingly sacrifice sleep to spend more time at work. Forty-three per cent said they were sacrificing sleep time to go on-line or watch TV, and 55 per cent of 18–29-year-olds confessed this is a chronic problem. One study showed 55 per cent of those under 25 involved in car crashes were suffering from sleep deprivation.[6]

Applause for Mark and Marjorie's busy life

Mark, a lawyer in Dallas, Texas, works 10 to 12 hours a day, often beginning at 5 or 6 am in order to have some time in the evenings for his family. But that time too is an incredible blur of activity as daughters who are challenged to be the best at everything are shuttled constantly from music lessons to soccer and basketball practice. On weekends Mark and his wife Marjorie dash to the mall to shop for the latest fashions then to the soccer field, to the basketball court and finally off to the local health club for their own weekly workout.

Marjorie and Mark are determined to model the "perfect Christian family". They live in a very upscale neighbourhood in Dallas and never like to miss church on Sunday. However this commitment is being eroded increasingly by the growing competition of Sunday morning soccer games for the kids. Marjorie often races into church ten or more minutes late and flops exhausted into the pew. She can rarely concentrate on the message and feels her spiritual life is slowly draining away. Mark is proud of his family's commitment to such a hectic schedule. He relishes the accolades of his friends and family, who constantly applaud his busy life while his entire family lives on the edge of exhaustion.

Mark and Marjorie, like too many of us, derive their sense of self-worth from outrageous busyness. "Stress has become a badge of honour of the millennium" stated Arlene Kagle, a psychologist who practises in Manhattan. "We lost the idea of the Sabbath as a day of rest long ago. Now we have lost evenings, nights and weekends as well ... Then we complain – that is to say brag – that we're just so wound up and tense we can barely sleep ..." [7] Sound familiar? Are you, your family or friends paying the high costs of your hurry sickness?

Diagnosing the cause of hurry sickness

Where does hurry sickness come from? Some people think it is simply a consequence of trying to crowd too much stuff into our already congested schedules. Of course that is part of it. Even those of us in Christian ministry can overdo it. In fact Christine wound up in the hospital in Tyler, Texas, in 1992 with Chronic Fatigue Syndrome as a consequence of trying to stretch herself too thinly while she was the Medical Director of Mercy Ships. Christine knows first hand how Elijah felt in 1 Kings 19 when he exhausted himself working for God's cause. But she also used her exhaustion as a time to encounter God and find renewal and refocusing, like Elijah did at Mount Horeb.

Do you want to find out why so many of us struggle with chronic hurry sickness? Then check out how we have bought into someone else's notion of what is best. When we allow others to define what is important and of value for us, that in turn defines where we spend our time and money.

For example, in spite of their genuine faith, we believe Mark and Marjorie have unwittingly allowed Boom City to define what is best for their family. Their incredible busyness, which they wear like a badge of honour, is a direct result of their notion of the good life. Mark's drivenness can be traced back to the need to get to the top of the ladder in his law practice, even though it leaves very little time for his family and spiritual life. Marjorie and her daughters' drivenness can be traced directly back to the need to excel in all the suburban competitions from endless youth achievement projects to consumer competition in fashions, furnishings, vehicles and vacations. Given the unstated mission statements to which this family has unwittingly committed their lives it shouldn't be surprising that they are suffering from hurry sickness.

Welcome to Boom City

As we race along the crowded highway of our lives both sides of the road are congested with huge, electronic, three-dimensional billboards all promising the land of wine and roses in a place called Boom City. Whether we recognize it or not, most of us have embraced someone's notion, consciously or unconsciously, of what constitutes the good life and better future.

Hurry sickness begins here. Whatever vision we embrace as the good life and better future determines what is really important to us. What is important to us directly determines where we spend our time and money. So identifying our intended destinations gives us a shot at not only understanding why we are so crazily busy ... but doing something about it.

It's tough on the frenetic motorway of life to decide which off ramp to take to find our way home to the best God has for us. Some destinations are vivid and inviting, others lie on obscure and hidden back roads. Even people of serious faith all over the planet often have trouble discerning whether Boom City is really the city of hope or a land of illusions. To really understand what Boom City offers us we need to understand its earliest beginnings.

Off Ramp No. 1

Hurry sickness audit time

Are you struggling with hurry sickness? Are you exhausted? Is your high pressure timestyle taking a toll on your family life, relationships and spiritual life? Do you sense that you are missing the best that God has for you? Is it possible that one of the major reasons you are over-booked is that you too have allowed others to define your sense of what is important and of value?

We invite you to leave the fast lane and pull off to a quiet spot, get a notebook or journal and get to work. This book will be much more valuable to you if you participate in every "off ramp" exercise. Open your notebook and answer the following questions:

1. Outline where you spent your time during the past week and your money during the past month.
2. Where are you feeling the greatest pressure on your time schedule and your budget?
3. Where are you paying the highest costs from hurry sickness in your health, your relationships with family and friends, in your involvement in your church and relationship to God? How motivated are you to make some changes?
4. Hurry sickness audit time. Based on where you spent your time and money, what are the aspirations and values that seem to drive your life and where do they come from? Is your life driven by the expectations of your workplace, your suburban community, your family, friends and neighbours? Try setting your answer to music or put it in poetic verse and sing it or read it along with your other answers to your study group or to a friend.

The storytellers of the Enlightenment told us a new story. They told us that if we co-operate with the laws governing the natural world all of society will automatically progress and life will get better and better. Construction of this gleaming metropolis actually began during the Enlightenment. Francis Bacon was one of its earliest architects. In his book, *The New Atlantis*, he sketched a vision of a technological paradise of affluence and unbelievable consumer choice. He assured us that this vision could be achieved through unleashing the power of science and technology to subdue the natural world and create a society of extraordinary comfort, security and wealth.

Essentially the storytellers of the Enlightenment took the vertical vision of the pursuit of the kingdom of God, that reigned during the Middle Ages, and tipped it on its side. Their focus became the horizontal vision of social progress, economic affluence and technological mastery. Today we call this dream the Western dream. This vision's notion of the good life is defined as getting ahead economically. It is a dream preoccupied exclusively with the here and now, focused on satisfying our needs for "more". This is the dream that both drives Boom City and makes it so attractive to many of us.

The industrial and cyber revolutions have made this gleaming city into a stunning reality. Boom City has emerged in modern society as much grander and more affluent than anything Bacon or those earliest architects ever imagined. Haven't you and your loved ones been enjoying life in this wonderland of "more"? Let's look at how Boom City is becoming an amazing global reality as we race into the 21st century.

In the nineties, as Tom explained in *Mustard Seed vs Mc World*, something altogether new happened to this city of affluence, technological innovation and incredible consumer choice ... it went global. When the Berlin wall came down and the Soviet Union imploded all the centrally planned Marxist economies were thrown into the rubbish bin of history because they didn't work very well. Virtually every nation on earth joined the free-market race to the top. The United States has enjoyed an unprecedented ten-year economic boom. But the horrific terrorist attack of 11 September 2001 tipped us into a new global recession, and no one knows how long it will last or how much pain there will be.

What made possible the creation of this one-world economic order was the girding of the planet with a global electronic nervous system of satellite dishes, fax machines and the internet. Through this nervous system $1.5 trillion circulates around the earth every day.[8] As Dorothy said to Toto in *The Wizard of Oz*, "I don't think we are in Kansas anymore!" And we aren't in the 70s, 80s or 90s anymore either. We have moved into a new neighbourhood that offers incredible new affluence and ever-expanding consumer choice.

We visited the Seattle Home Show recently and caught a glimpse of this amazing new booming global economy. There were over 100 hot tub dealers. We wondered how Seattle, with a population of some one million occupants could support that many hot tub businesses. Then we remembered we live in Microsoft land where not only Bill Gates but hundreds of other new millionaires are building 20,000 to 40,000 square foot mansions ... complete with four to six hot tubs plus lavish second homes also equipped with hot tubs. In the past decade we have seen the creation of more jobs and rising wages. Growing numbers of the poor have come off welfare and gone back to work.[9] The

New York Times has heralded the economic boom as "the best of times".[10] And a host of articles in business magazines trumpet it simply doesn't get any better than this! Are you among those doing better?

As Boom City goes global, everywhere is beginning to look like everywhere else with all the same upscale shops, tourist accommodations and franchised fast food outlets. But Boom City is above all else a global 24/7 shopping mall ... on-line all the time.[11] Internet shopping gives the consumer a remarkable opportunity to shop in the Boom City Mall for bargains literally from all over the world. One of the amazing aspects of this boom economy is that soon we will have the opportunity to design our own cars, furniture and wardrobes on-line. Many of us are experiencing a new unprecedented level of individual consumer choice.

In the creation of this new one-world economic order we have seen an absolute explosion of wealth for the top 20 per cent. More billionaires and millionaires were created in the past ten years than at any time in human history. Trump World Towers at United Nations Plaza in New York offers apartments with a panoramic view at the bargain basement prices of $13,400,000.[12] Builders can hardly keep up with the booming demand for yachts and the bigger the better. Titanic luxury at only $13 million.[13] Such a deal!

"I wanna be a gazillionaire geek"

Millionaire mania has gone global. Many countries now have some version of the explosively popular game show "Who wants to be a millionaire?".[14] In the United States an array of new shows continue to spin off. Some call it the "Millionaire effect". The motorways are congested with millions intent on crowding the wide off ramp headed towards this new Shangri-La of spectacular wealth and extravagant consumer choice.

"Why work for General Motors or anybody else when you can invent your own company, get rich and retire before you're 30?" Students at Massachusetts Institute of Technology's Sloan School of Business asked this question when 150 teams gathered for a unique competition to decide the best plan for new business start-ups. The contest is called "I Wanna Be a Gazillionaire Geek" and often those who win find venture capitalists ready to fund their start-ups. One of the recent winners was DirectHit, a web-research technology firm that helps users identify the most popular sites. This student project has actually attracted $1.5 million in investment as a new start-up.[15]

Of course not everyone wants to be a gazillionaire. Many people tell us they would be satisfied if they had just a little more money or a little more security than they have now. But when people do see a sudden increase in their income it is only a question of time before they are discontented again. While the scripture encourages us to be content in whatever situation we find ourselves the architects of Boom City are committed to persuading us to be chronically discontented.

Boosting for Boom City

So many people are doing well economically it's not hard to find boosters for Boom City. John Micklethwait and Adrian Wooldndge make a strong case in their book, *A Future Perfect*, that this new one-world economic order is indeed that much sought after El Dorado. They argue:

"The simple fact is that globalization makes us richer or makes enough of us richer to make the whole process worthwhile."[16] Are they right? Is the ultimate really defined in terms of economic freedom and individual choice? Is this new boom economy of rising affluence and ever-expanding consumer choice the real promised land or is it a land of illusions?

Hidden price tags for life in Boom City

"A very modern mood disorder has settled over the most prosperous nation there ever was. On the crest of the boom, there is sadness. In a time of peace, there is anxiety. Amidst unprecedented stimulation, there is boredom. Just what is going on? ... The paradox can be lost on no one: America is enjoying unprecedented levels of prosperity, health care, life expectancy, food supply and peace. ('Things aren't just getting better,' as Sir John Tempelton put in his latest book, *Is Progress Speeding Up? Our Multiplying Multitudes of Blessings*, 'they're getting better and better at a faster and faster rate.') Yet it's suffering unprecedented rates of depression."[17]

If the boosters of Boom City are right, and everything is "getting better and better at a faster and faster rate" why aren't we having a better time? Why are so many of us afflicted by hurry sickness, stress and depression? Without a doubt we do live in the most affluent period in human history where the greatest number are sharing in the bounty of a huge range of consumer delectables. But what the boosters of Boom City fail to mention is that there are some huge hidden price tags for life in this city of palatial wealth and incredible choice.

In our efforts to find the best many of us have been taken in by the extremely seductive advertisements along the freeway. Is the good life really all about getting a bigger piece of the rock and enjoying the delights of Boom City or is something else? Just what are the hidden price tags we are paying for the good life offered to, us by the marketers of Boom City?

Price tag number one for the British middle class is plummeting savings rates and soaring bankruptcy. Apparently we are bingeing out of our savings and other people's money.

Tammy and Rob have been married for two years. They desperately want to settle down, start a family and take some time for short-term missions too. But they can't do either. Every penny goes to pay off student loans and enormous credit card debts Rob incurred before marriage. Rob explained, "I thought credit cards would take over where my parents left off. It really never occurred to me I would actually have to pay for my clothes, car and CDs. I naively thought I could go on borrowing money forever." Fortunately they have set a strict budget and they are beginning to climb out. But many others aren't as successful in turning their situation around.

Why are so many of us, like Rob, enjoying the bounty of Boom City in a way that threatens our very future? Answer: we have bought Boom City's message of discontent that we will never find the satisfaction we seek unless we keep on consuming whether we can afford it or not. How have we succumbed to this message that encourages us to be chronically discontented?

Until the early 1920s people only bought what they needed ... the essentials of life – food to eat, clothes to wear and a roof over their heads. However, it was clear to business leaders of the day that if they simply sold people what they needed they wouldn't do much business so they created a fifth human need ... the need for novelty. The marketers of Boom City convinced us that meeting our basic needs isn't enough ... we must constantly be persuaded to buy the newest and the latest novelty to be successful human beings. Buchanan calls this addiction "The Cult of the Next Thing". "The Cult of the Next Thing proclaims, 'Crave and spend for the Kingdom of stuff is here'. It teaches that our lives are measured in the abundance of our possessions."[18]

In recent years these marketers have even convinced many of us that we are what we own and the more we own the more we are. They have actually persuaded us that our very identity and self-worth comes from the cars we drive, the neighbourhoods we live in and the brands we proudly wear. In fact we have become a society of unpaid walking advertisements for branded products. Incredibly there is a church in Phoenix, Arizona, that has even allowed itself to become branded with a corporate logo.

To make matters worse in this new global economy shareholders do not want 3 per cent to 5 per cent return on investment. They want 10 per cent, 15 per cent, or even 25 per cent if they can get it. The only way that is possible is for all of us, and particularly our kids, to consume at levels never seen before on this planet. We must constantly be convinced that yesterday's luxuries have become today's necessities. And the more we are persuaded to spend on our expensive lifestyles the more hours we will need to work which, as you will see, directly contributes to our hurry sickness ... big time.

Long hours, conspicuous consumption

When we work with Christians in Britain, Canada, the United States, Australia and New Zealand we always ask the same question: "How many feel you are working harder and longer than a few years ago?" Invariably 70 per cent raise their hands. A report published by the TUC in 1999 showed that Britons work the longest hours in Europe – an average of 44 hours a week as compared to 39 in Holland, Belgium and Denmark and there is growing pressure on workers to work longer hours.[19] In 1977 less than half of families in Europe and North America relied on dual incomes. Today it has increased dramatically to two-thirds and is still climbing. Some women work simply to help pay the mounting bills and keep their families' heads above water. But growing numbers are working to satisfy our rapidly expanding appetites for more.[20]

In the US a new phenomenon is emerging, the four-income family. According to *Money Magazine* "Simply put it can now take four – or more – jobs to provide the level of comfort and financial security that one income delivered a few decades ago." As we have already seen growing numbers are a part of a new 24/7[21] labour force that never gets away from work. Do you find yourself or members of your family in this picture?

The message from Boom City is that our sense of identity, self-worth and purpose for life come not only from what we buy but also from where we work. Not only men but increasingly women seem to derive their greatest sense of purpose and personal identity from their jobs. Australian commentator Bob Santamaria declares that our new boom global economy has declared war on the family. He asserts that financial and work pressures of this highly demanding new economy are directly contributing to escalating family breakups.[22] Families need help here!

High price tags of Boom City for the young

The marketers of Boom City realized in the nineties that if they were to keep this boom economy booming they had to get all of us, but particularly the young, to consume at levels never seen before. In the documentary film *Affluenza*[23] we are shown a marketing executive training other marketing professionals. He challenges them, "You have to get kids branded by age 5 if you want to have their product loyalty for their entire lives." If you have ever tried to get a 5-year-old past McDonalds you know how successful they are. Gary Ruskin in an article in Mothering magazine exposes this effort by marketers to target our kids. He explains "If you own this child at an early age, you can own this child for years to come."[24] And both children and families are succumbing to this marketing pressure on the young to consume at levels never seen before. Have you experienced this pressure on the young?

Kids want more entertainment too. Reportedly the average American child is on-line 37 hours a week ... TV, MTV, CDs, video games, internet chat rooms. And they are exposed to 3,000 to 4,000 advertisements a week. And that number is increasing as corporations invade both public and private schools with inexpensive curriculum that includes their corporate ads. "Advertising is a type of curriculum – the most pervasive in America today ... They teach that the solutions to life's problems lie not in good values, hard work, or education, but in materialism and the purchasing of more and more things."[25] And we have seen evidence of this same phenomenon across the Western world from New Zealand to Norway.

Teenagers, too, are a major target for the branders of Boom City. Programmed to believe their very identity comes from being cool, they spend every waking minute trying to fit in, wear the right brands and portray the right image to their peers. "This was not a time for selling Tide and Snuggle to housewives", says Canadian activist Naomi Klein in speaking of the marketing strategies of the 1990s. "It was a time for beaming MTV, Nike, Hilfiger, Microsoft, Netscape and Wired to global teens and their overgrown imitators ... Through this process, peer pressure emerged as a powerful market force, making the keeping-up-with-the Joneses consumerism of their suburban parents pale by comparison. As clothing retailer Elise Decotèau said of her teen shoppers, 'They run in packs. If you sell to one, you sell to everyone in their class and everyone in their school."[26] "Clique uniformity" and "social corralling" are the new reality for branded teens.[27]

Surprising numbers of parents are even caving in to their teens' demands for cosmetic surgery for everything from breast enlargement to liposuction.[28] The message of what's best in Boom City for all generations couldn't be clearer ... it's all about individual gratification: "Got the urge?", "Is your mouth ready?", "Pamper yourself", "Seize the moment!", "Fortune smiles on you", "You deserve a break today!", "I will live my life on my terms!"

Extreme cool and high status

While conducting a church retreat in Olympia, Washington, we divided participants into two groups: those under 35 and those over 35. We asked the younger group to identify what is "extreme cool" in terms of where they shop, the brands they wear and what they drive. Their list included shopping at the Gap and Banana Republic, wearing cool brands like Tommy Hilfiger, Old Navy and Nike and driving cool cars like Jeeps, Jettas, and HUMVs. The over 35s had a little different idea of what constituted "high status": shopping at Nordstroms, brands like Ralph Lauren, Brooks Brothers and Calvin Klein, buying a waterfront home on the edge of Lake Washington in Bill Gates' neighbourhood, driving a Lexus, Saturn or SUV (Sports Utility Vehicle) with all the extras, and luxury cruise line vacations. Many of them expressed surprise at how important these items had become in their lives. One young woman candidly confessed that she needed to shop almost every day for clothes to be acceptable to her friends. Regardless of your income do you and your kids feel some of the pressure to achieve extreme cool and high status?

As we speed along the motorways of life there is a dawning realization for some that Boom City may not be the promised land and getting all the stuff may not be the good life after all. Many of us both inside and outside the church are discovering the land of affluence may indeed be a land of illusions. In the film *The Truman Show*, Christof, the producer of the imaginary world in which Truman lives, is asked why Truman has not discovered that his world is make-believe. He responds: "We accept the reality of the world with which we're presented." In another popular film, *The Matrix*, Morpheus describes the Matrix – the imaginary world in which human beings are living as "The world that has been pulled over your eyes to blind you from the truth." Have many of us, like the characters in these films, accepted Boom City's notion of reality and vision of the good life ... no questions asked?

Of course most of us aren't living palatially. We are simply trying to make ends meet. But we still tend to buy into Boom City's notion of what constitutes happiness. Christian parents want what's best for their kids but too often we too, like those outside the faith, define what is best in terms of getting ahead economically. Are we simply the sum of the work we do and the things we buy or are we something more? Is happiness simply the sum of economic success for us and our kids or is it something more? Is it possible we are missing the best that God has for us?

David Myers, a psychologist at Hope College, asks "After four decades of rising affluence ... are we happier ... than before? We are not. Since 1957 the number of Americans who say they are 'very happy' has declined from 35 to 32 per cent. Meanwhile, the divorce rate has doubled, the teen suicide rate has nearly tripled ... and more people than ever (particularly young adults) are depressed. I call this soaring wealth and shrinking spirit 'the American paradox'. More than ever we have big houses and broken homes, high incomes and low morale ... In an age of plenty, we feel spiritual hunger."[29]

Branded for life

What has happened, we believe, is that we haven't just moved into Boom City, Boom City has moved into us. More than we recognize, Boom City has branded us and defined, even for people of vital faith, what is important and what is of value. We have unwittingly allowed Boom

City to write the mission statement for our lives and families, but few of us seemed to notice. The Bible reminds us that "we are in the world but not of the world." We can't physically move out of this new booming consumer culture but we can move it out of us. We can reject the idolatry of acquisitiveness, covetousness and the pursuit of individual upscaling.

Paul outlines how all the followers of Jesus can get out of the fast lane and find God's best. "... I urge ... in view of God's mercy, to offer your bodies as living sacrifices, holy and pleasing to God – this is your spiritual act of worship. Do not conform any longer to the pattern of this world, but be transformed by the renewing of your mind. Then you will be able to test and approve what God's will is – his good, pleasing and perfect will" (Romans 12:1–2). We will only find God's best when we refuse to conform any longer to the aspirations and values of Boom City and invite God to transform our inmost sense of what is important and of value which will in turn change the direction and tempo of our lives.

Boom City – finding your way out of town

Paul and Fiona Johnson found a way to move Boom City out of their lives and connect to a very different story and a very different view of what is best. At a seminar Christine held at Spring Harvest, she helped participants including Fiona and Paul to write a beginning biblical mission statement. The Johnsons returned home to Bristol and used their mission statement to reprioritize their entire lives. With a struggle they gave up some of the consumer addictions that were stressing

Off Ramp No. 2

High status and extreme cool audit time

 Come with us to another off ramp and bring your notebook or journal. Try to answer the following questions as candidly as possible:

1. If you are over 35, what is high status in your community ... in terms of the most desirable places to live, the most prestigious jobs, the places to shop, the brands people wear, the vehicles they drive, the places they holiday, prestige kid activity and the premier schools for the young?

2. If you are under 35, what is extreme cool among people your age in terms of the brands they wear, the places they shop, the places they go, the cars they drive, the technology they use, the most prestigious jobs and the places they holiday?

3. Now get out your old magazines, scissors and glue and create a large collage of pictures, ads and words that playfully portray what is extreme cool or high status in your community.

4. High status, extreme cool audit time. To what extent do you honestly find your sense of what is best really comes from Boom City's notion of extreme cool and high status? Share your list, your pictorial montage and your candid confession of your struggle with your study group or a good friend ... and pray to find God's best for your life.

out both their budget and their time schedule. They carved out daily time for scripture study and prayer where they had very little time before. They set aside more weekly family time to enjoy their two kids. Fiona and Paul also set aside two hours a week to visit a local nursing home, where their kids read to the seniors. They began to discover, as many others have, that the good life of God is a life given away. The Johnsons also freed up more time for hospitality, treating their friends to food they love cooking from all over the world. Paul and Fiona tell us that they are enjoying the serious beginning they have made to find God's best for their lives and family.

If you want to join the Johnsons in finding a less stressed, more festive, way of life that counts for something, join us in the next chapter. We will discover in an ancient story and a future hope a new sense of purpose for our lives and loved ones. Remember when two disciples walked with Christ along the Emmaus road and they were so preoccupied that they didn't even recognize Jesus? Some of us are so preoccupied with our busy lives and the attractions of Boom City that we are missing both that personal encounter with God as well as the best that God has for us. Our God loves us very much and longs to set us free from our driven lives and help us find a way of life with a difference. That journey begins, as we will see, by rediscovering our place in God's story and with that a new compelling sense of direction for our lives.

Notes

[1] *Discipleship Journal*, Issue 60, November/December 1990, p. 23.
[2] John Ortberg, *The Life You've Always Wanted*, Grand Rapids: Zondervan Publishers, 1997, p. 82.
[3] Ortberg, p. 84.

[4] Katie Hafner, "For the Well Connected, All the World's an Office", *New York Times*, March 30, 2000, pp. D1 & D7.

[5] Annetta Miller, "The Millennium Mind-Set: It's Here, It's Clear, Get Used to It", *American Demographics*, January 1999, p. 63.

[6] Mary Harvey, "Sleepless in America", *American Demographics*, July 2000, pp. 9–10.

[7] Joanne Kaufman, "What's the Best Thing About Stress? There's Plenty of It", *New York Times*, June 25, 2000, p. 4.

[8] Tom Sine, *Mustard Seed vs Mc World: Reinventing Life and Faith for the Future* (London: Monarch Books, 1999).

[9] "Good Ble$$ America", *Christianity Today*, April 3, 2000, p. 34.

[10] Peter D. Sutherland and John W. Sewell, "Gathering the Nations to Promote Globalization", *New York Times*, February 8, 1998, p. 1.

[11] Kathleen Madigan and David Lindorif, "Consumers Have Money to Burn", *Business Week*, April 20, 1998, pp. 42–43.

[12] Jerry Adler and Tara Weingarten, "Mansions Off the Rack", *Newsweek*, February 14, 2000, p. 60.

[13] Craig Wilson, "Size Does Matter", *USA Today*, July 7, 2000, p. D1.

[14] Barry Bearak, "Many, Many in India Want to Be a Millionaire", *New York Times*, August 30, 2000, p. 1.

[15] Donna Foote, "Show Us the Money", *Newsweek*, April 19, 1999, pp. 43–45.

[16] John Micklethwait and Adrian Wooldridge, *A Future Perfect: The Challenge and Hidden Promise of Globalization*, New York: Crown Business, 2000, p. 335.

[17] Kalle Lasn and Bruce Grierson, "Malignant Sadness", *Adbusters*, June / July 2000, pp. 28–35.

[18] Mark Buchanan, "The Cult of the Next Thing", *The Covenant Companion*, November 2000, p. 7.

[19] BBC News Online: "Business: The Economy", August 26, 1999.

[20] Tamar Lewin, "Men Assuming Bigger Share At Home New Survey Shows", *New York Times*, April 15, 1998, p. A16.

[21] Lesley Alderman, "Here Comes the four-income family", *Money Magazine*, Feb 1995, p. 1. The term 24/7 is used as a metaphor for the modern lifestyle where people are often expected to be on call 24 hours a day, 7 days a week.

[22] Bob Santamaria, "The Global Economy – At War with the Family", *Humanity*, July 1998, p. 6.

[23] *Affluenza*, a documentary coproduced by KCTS/Seattle and Oregon Public Broadcasting 1997.

[24] Gary Ruskin, "Why They Whine: How Corporations Prey on Children", *Mothering* magazine, Nov/Dec 1999, p. 42.

[25] Ruskin, p. 43.

[26] Naomi Klein, *No Logo*, Canada: Alfred A. Knopf Publishers, 2000, p. 68.

[27] Adrian Nicole LeBlanc, "The Tyranny Of Cool", *New York Times* magazine, November 14, 1999, pp. 94–96.

[28] Robert D. Putnam, *Bowling Alone: The Collapse and Renewal of American Community*, New York: Simon & Schuster, 2000, p. 260.

[29] David G. Myers, "Wealth, Well-Being, and the New American Dream", *Enough: A Quarterly Report on Consumption, the Quality of Life and the Environment*, no. 12, Summer 2000, p. 5.

Travels with a Primate

Terry Waite

From darkest Africa to the darker and infinitely wetter birthplace of John Knox, from the remote expanse of the Alaska Highway to parts of the Antipodes that even Bill Bryson could not reach, Terry Waite takes us on a guided tour across the globe in the company of Dr Robert Runcie.

Even an Archbishop has little control over wars and missed connections, floods and food poisoning, but this Primate sails majestically through the most troubled of waters, as his companions bale energetically in his wake.

Travels with a Primate is the hilarious and affectionate story of the trials and tribulations they encounter, and a delightful tribute to an enduring friendship.

HarperCollins Religious
ISBN: 0-00-710633-5

Price: £7.99

£5.99 with voucher

First published in 2000 by HarperCollins Religious
77 – 85 Fulham Palace Road, Hammersmith,
London, W6 8JB

4

The Hog Farm

'The Bronx. No thonx.' So said Ogden Nash. 'USA. No way,' was my own less than worthy feeling when it was suggested that a visit to the Episcopal Church in the United States ought to be arranged.

It was not that I disliked the United States. Far from it. I first visited that vast country as a young man and was greatly appreciative of the generosity I experienced there. In fact, I first met the Revd Sam in New York. He was labouring away in the Head Office of the Episcopal Church on Second Avenue. His task in those days was to see that American Churchmen around the world were properly cared for. This particular work demanded not only diplomatic skill but also considerable stamina, as he frequently had to visit lone American missionaries toiling in some remote corner of the global vineyard. Eventually he came to visit us in Uganda and brought us news of others working in Japan, Southern Africa and South America. He was a frequent visitor to these far-flung regions, wherever the American Episcopal Church had interests.

My reservations about the USA were to do with the very size of the country Given the fact that so many MPs were anxious to listen to Dr Runcie proclaim the Christian message throughout the British Isles, clearly he could not be away for too long without doing damage to their immortal souls. America, being a large country; would take a great deal of time to visit properly.

Before undertaking the journey to the New World, therefore, I consulted with our resident American in London, the aforementioned Revd Sam. This was in the days before the great silver auction and his office was still in desirable Westminster. It was not too easy to find, because, you will recollect, there was a certain amount of secrecy surrounding the Anglican Consultative Council. Those in the know, however, could locate it easily enough.

I have frequently marvelled at the ability of certain individuals to convey the impression that you are the *only* person they want to see that day. The Revd Sam was such a character. He swept me into his cheerful office, radiating enthusiasm. The walls were decorated with a few trophies marking his visits to the Orient, where the American Church had considerable interests. There were also several happy family photographs: Sam with 400 bishops, Sam with His Grace of Canterbury, Sam stepping into a taxi to meet with the Primus of Scotland and his bishops (that is, I do not mean to suggest that the good Primus and his Episcopal merry men were *all* in the taxi – although, come to think of it, they might well have been, as there are not too many Anglican Bishops in Scotland).

Although an American through and through, Sam invariably adjusted to his immediate surroundings with ease. I have watched him eat mashed boiled banana in Kenya as though it were the staple food of New Yorkers. Therein, I would suggest, lies the secret of his great diplomatic ability – namely empathy.

'Have a cup of tea?' he said. Tea and digestive biscuits arrived immediately.

'How was the Scottish meeting?' I enquired. (Dr Runcie and I, of course, had left Sam's meeting early in order to dine with the Moderator.)

'Very good,' said Sam with redoubled enthusiasm. 'Wonderful spirit.'

I marvelled then as I marvel now. There are certain exceptional individuals in this troubled world who have an unusual ability to enjoy conferences. Sam was such a man. His enjoyment so conveyed itself to others that they too came away from discussing the New Zealand Prayer Book, or a fresh administrative region for the Church in Borneo, and (as it were) danced through the streets of Dundee.

'The next full meeting of the ACC will be in Nigeria as you know,' he said. 'They have a splendid new government conference centre, but more about that later. You're off to America soon, aren't you?'

I had seen many such government centres in Africa and needed some convincing of their attractiveness. Leaving such quibbles aside for the time being, however, I agreed that the United States was my concern at this particular moment.

'You can't go everywhere, obviously,' he said, 'but you must cover as much ground as possible – 815 will want a visit; you must go to rural America and, of course, to California. The White House should be on the programme also.'

The '815' to which the Revd Sam referred was not, as one might imagine, another secret HQ. It was the address on Second Avenue where the Episcopal Church in the United States had its main administrative office and, above which the Presiding Bishop resided in a penthouse. (I should explain that the Presiding Bishop was the top man in the Episcopal Church, equal with such individuals as the Primus, Archbishop Timothy, and a host of other characters whom we have yet to encounter.)

We often hear that what America does today, the remainder of the world does tomorrow. There is a certain amount of truth in this statement. The Episcopal Church was first into the great auction business, and began to sell off the family heirlooms when ordinary folk still thought that a bailiff was but a rural farmworker in the old country. The magnificent residence and offices of the Presiding Bishop in Greenwich, Connecticut were rapidly disposed of in favour of 815. The poor old PB, as he was affectionately called, was forced to move to Second Avenue and live above the shop. Being a holy man, he accepted this change without complaint. 'Penthouse' may sound very grand, but in reality it was just a top-floor flat with a couple of guest rooms tacked on.

Fuelled by our tea and digestive biscuits, the Revd Sam and I roughed out a draft programme for the proposed archiepiscopal visit to the States. One year later, I sat with Dr Runcie and his Chaplain in the much-maligned penthouse high above Second Avenue.

Generally speaking, in the days when it was my good fortune to travel with Dr Runcie, his fellow Archbishops throughout the world were a good-natured bunch. The PB in America was certainly one of the most amiable. I imagine that a certain theatrical ability is required in order to appear in church Sunday by Sunday and entertain the faithful, but the PB'S real talent was displayed when, accompanied by none other than the Revd Sam on the piano, he performed a most acceptable rendering of the old song, 'In the five and ten cent store'. I hasten to add that he did not, of course, sing this ditty in church, but at private social gatherings. As he was certainly no show-off, he took not a little persuading to display his vocal talents, but when he did so it was always appreciated.

The PB was briefing us on the details of the programme that had been roughed out so long ago. 'We've included a visit I know you'll enjoy,' he said, as Dr Runcie stood on the balcony of the penthouse mopping his brow. It was very hot and humid. A fire engine ploughed its way through the evening rush-hour traffic making a noise like a wounded rhinoceros.

'It's a bit noisy out here,' observed the Archbishop, as the air-conditioning outlet blasted into action. We moved indoors and silence fell as the PB closed the triple-glazed doors. A noticeable chill descended on the room, as though by some miracle we had been transported 'to the territory covered by the Bishop of the Arctic.

'It's not easy to get the balance right,' said the PB as he fiddled with the air-conditioner. He gave up, settled into a comfortable sofa and returned to the matter in hand. 'The visit you'll enjoy is to a hog farm.'

Those who have stumbled across this book and are reading about the everyday life of Archbishops for the first time may be a little surprised that such a location would figure on a visit by His Grace to our American cousins. In fact, there should be no surprise. The Archbishop of Canterbury had a well-known fondness for pigs, Berkshires in particular. He claimed to have owned several of the species, and it was with a heavy heart that he gave them to a charity when the demands of office became too great.

My knowledge of hogs was certainly not as extensive as that of the Archbishop. It was limited to the days when, as a boy, I watched them being fed in my home village on a repulsive mixture known as Manchester Pudding. The mixture was composed of scraps collected from various hotels in the Manchester area. The scraps were boiled and then fed to the grateful swine in huge, evil-smelling chunks. From time to time, an item of cutlery from the Midland Hotel or another such grand establishment was discovered in the mix, and we would know who to blame for that week's appalling aroma.

The Archbishop duly expressed pleasure at the thoughtful inclusion of pigs in his itinerary, and the PB was gratified. The following morning we departed for rural America.

The hog farm we visited was on a somewhat grander scale that the humble establishment I had. known in my youth. I remember from those days a makeshift little pen with a couple of porkers anxiously awaiting whatever fare the finest Manchester eating houses could provide. America, as, ever, was bigger and better – a thousand times so.

When we landed at the airport, the hog farmer met us with his private helicopter. 'Hi!' he said cheerfully. To my untrained eye, he looked like a mid-western banker – and that, I discovered, was exactly what he was. He owned the largest hog farm in the country and the most prestigious bank in the state.

As we flew across the flatlands, he shouted information at us. The noise of the helicopter was such that it was only possible to catch occasional words. 'Automatic feed … 20,000 every day … world hunger … hygiene …'

We nodded dutifully while the Chaplain scribbled away in a notebook. The hog farmer, imagining that he was taking notes, kept the information flowing, in fact, the Chaplain was conscious that on the morrow Dr Runcie had to deliver at least five major speeches, of which only three had so far been drafted. It was necessary for him to redeem the time, as they say

The pilot of the helicopter circled. Below us we could see a complex that resembled one of the larger British holiday camps. We put down in the midst of the compound and were greeted by a whole group of porcine bankers. A hay cart had been decked out with some bunting and a microphone, and Dr Runcie was encouraged to clamber aboard and deliver some well-chosen words, which he did with his usual eloquence. There was a little polite applause and then a man approached us dressed as though he was about to perform major surgery He was clad from head to toe in white; he wore a white cap and his features were cloaked in a white protective mask. I imagined that the hogs felt quite safe in his presence.

'You need to put these on,' he muttered through the gauze, while he handed us three pairs of white overalls. We obediently changed and were ushered towards a couple of electric golf carts for a tour of the establishment. We saw a lot of hogs, that I can guarantee. Clearly they were superior hogs, who had never heard of Manchester Pudding, let alone tasted it.

At the conclusion of the tour, the hog banker took us to one side for some refreshment. 'I have a scheme,' he said, 'that will change the world.' Dr Runcie looked interested, as changing the world was something dear to his heart. 'I want you, Archbishop,' the banker went on with a flourish, 'to take one of my best hogs to England. I want you, Archbishop, to breed that hog. I want you, Archbishop, to send lots of little hogs to Africa. If you do that, we will solve the problem of world hunger.'

The Archbishop needed no convincing. It was a good scheme. Feed a hog, breed a hog, and send the little ones to a warmer climate. There and then we went to see our hog, Martha.

Alas, it was several months before the plan could come to fruition. Bureaucrats can put the damper on the most promising of schemes. Who would need convincing that American hogs were in robust health? The Ministry Who was reluctant to allow the finest hog in the world into England? The Ministry Who insisted that the most wonderful hog in America had to spend months in quarantine? The Ministry Finally, however, the great day dawned and Martha emerged from months of isolation into the welcoming company of His Grace of Canterbury By now all the other archiepiscopal hogs had gone to be cared for elsewhere and Martha joined them. Never one 'to forget old friends, the Archbishop visited them frequently.

Sad to say, world hunger is still with us and no little archiepiscopal piglets ever saw the sunny shores of Africa. Why not? Well, Martha proved to be infertile. I do not know if this disastrous news was ever communicated to the hog banker in America. I suspect it may not have been. He meant well. Everyone meant well.

The Chaplain, always one to subject any scheme to the most cynical scrutiny, was not impressed. 'What,' he said, quoting an old proverb, 'what can you expect from a pig but a grunt?'

'Animals can be soothing,' I replied. 'Remember the limerick?'

> 'An Archbishop, to keep himself calm,
> Kept pigs on a Hertfordshire farm.
> The grunts and the snores
> Of the prize-winning boars
> To episcopal ears were as balm.'

The Chaplain did not grunt. He was too much of a gentle-man for that. He simply returned to his scribbling without a further word.

★ ★ ★ ★ ★

Those who have followed these stories so far will have developed some familiarity with the Anglican Consultative Council. They will know that the ACC was composed of Bishops, clergy and laymen and -women from across the globe. They will further know that the one who ensured that the Council met on time and dutifully worked through its agenda was none other than the Revd Sam. I have hinted, too, that there was a slight air of secrecy about the Council. Any reader can test this simply by button-holing an ordinary member of any Anglican church throughout the world and questioning them about the ACC. I guarantee you a blank look and shuffling of the feet.

There is, however, an even more clandestine body that congregates from time to time, and this is known as the Primates' Meeting. In Anglican circles the Primus of Scot-land, Archbishop Timothy, the PB of America, His Grace of Canterbury and several others are all known as Primates. Every few years or so they meet together, with Canterbury in the chair and the Revd Sam in attendance, shuffling not his feet but a sheaf of papers.

During the travels of Dr Runcie through the New World, Primates from across the Communion had made their way to America and were planning to deliberate at the College of Preachers in Washington. Dr Runcie was due to join them for a day or so (provided he could tear himself away from the hogs).

The College of Preachers nestles in the shadow of what is called The National Cathedral in Washington. This

impressive looking Anglican edifice is built along classical
lines and attempts to play a significant role in American life
similar to that played by Westminster Abbey or St Paul's
Cathedral in the United Kingdom. The College of
Preachers is not, as some cynics might fondly imagine, a
contemporary manifestation of the Tower of Babel. It is a
conference centre where, from time to time, clerics and
others are instructed in the art of sermonizing. It is normally a place that I would avoid at all costs. Duty called,
however.

By the time we arrived, the other Primates were well
established and very much at home. They had flown in
from across the globe and were being greeted by our genial
and hospitable preaching hosts. I shall not dwell on the
conference itself, for the simple reason that I have not the
slightest recollection what these excellent men discussed
during their days together. I could hazard a guess. The
Lambeth Conference of Bishops might have been mentioned. The creation of a new territory for the Anglican
Church somewhere in the world was bound to be an item.
The truth is that, then as now, these matters failed to grip
my attention and they have happily faded from memory

There is one event that remains clear, however, and that
is our afternoon visit to the White House. For some
extraordinary reason, many Archbishops and Bishops seem
to enjoy travelling together. Perhaps they feel there is safety
in numbers, or perhaps it is simply that the flock instinct
comes naturally to shepherds. If nothing else, of course, a
Bishop is less likely to get lost if there is someone with him
to check the tickets.

I am reminded of one young man who lived in Washington and invited his elderly aunt in England to visit him.
He told her that she was to buy a ticket that deposited her

at Dulles International airport, where he would meet her. 'Phone me when you get to the airport,' he said casually He was somewhat taken aback when his aunt did phone him. She said he was not to worry about collecting her. She would take a taxi. 'Where exactly are you?' he queried. 'Dallas, of course,' she replied. Bishops have similarly unworldly tendencies, believe me.

On the day of the visit to the White House, the Chaplain and I boarded the coach along with the Revd Sam and several dozen Archbishops. Had there been an accident, the whole Anglican Communion might be very different today There was no trouble, however, and we arrived safely. The White House security staff, although expecting this divine gathering, were nevertheless a little startled at the sight of so much purple. The clerics had donned their best garments for the visit. We were ushered cautiously through the gates. There was a slight disappointment, as the President had recently been shot. Not fatally, I am glad to say, but the injuries he sustained were sufficient to ensure that he remained in California, leaving the running of the shop to his deputy.

The party was greeted at the main door by a senior official wearing a very sharp suit and an equally incisive smile. The Archbishop, the Chaplain and myself were ushered to one side for a private conversation with the Vice President (as I have mentioned previously, Canterbury, although equal with other Archbishops, was head boy and thus received occasional treats) while the others were taken on a guided tour of this rather small but interesting building. Official secrets being what they are, I am obliged to pass over the details of that private conversation, although I can reveal that the meeting was cordial and that gifts were exchanged.

The Chaplain and I were in charge of the Archbishop's gifts, and a great nuisance they were too. Prior to any visit abroad, two large cases were stocked with a variety of trinkets. There were glass goblets engraved with a picture of Canterbury Cathedral, tiny enamel pillboxes bearing a coloured picture of Lambeth Palace, numerous signed photographs of His Grace decked out in his best Sunday kit, religious medallions – in fact, all the sort of stuff that has been the stock in trade of religious leaders across the generations. In return for these knick-knacks, we accumulated the most remarkable collection of paraphernalia you can possibly imagine. It was always a puzzle to know what to do with the stuff once it was back in Lambeth Palace, but more about that later.

We had naturally brought with us a most suitable gift for the White House. I know readers will find this all very unsatisfactory but once again I have completely forgotten what it was. It was certainly a superior gift and not a coloured tea towel or some other such trifle. I can say that with confidence, as we would certainly have wanted our esteem for the President of the United States to be reflected in the gift we were to offer. Before our departure from the White House, it (whatever it was) was duly handed over. The grateful recipient expressed much pleasure and beckoned to an aide, with whom he had a whispered conversation. The aide left the room and returned a moment or so later bearing an extremely handsome box.

'The President is so very sorry not to be here today,' said our acting host. (As he had recently been shot and wounded, we felt the President had a respectable excuse.) 'But before you leave he would like you to have this personal gift, Archbishop.'

He handed the box over and, like a participant in a quiz show, the Archbishop was encouraged to open it there and then. He did so and it was his turn to express extreme pleasure as he pulled a glass jar from the box.

'You will have seen that the President has an identical jar on his desk in the Oval Office,' said the Vice President. 'He keeps jellybeans in it.'

The Archbishop blinked. He had not seen jellybeans since he was a boy in Liverpool. The jar was returned to its box and handed across to the Chaplain for safekeeping. The Chaplain, a diplomat of the highest order, remained impassive throughout this moving exchange of valuables. Only those who knew him well would have been aware of his private thoughts about the priceless object.

Farewells were said, sentiments of goodwill were exchanged, and we were reunited with our band of purple-clad brothers. The Chaplain remained unusually silent during the journey back to our lodgings.

A week later, safely back within the walls of Lambeth Palace, we unpacked the gifts amassed during the Archbishop's American tour. The usual collection of diocesan shields, engraved scrolls and coffee mugs made their appearance. 'By the way,' I said. 'Where's the famous jellybean jar?'

The Chaplain did not reply immediately. When he did, it was in a cheerful manner. 'You didn't hear, my dear Terry?' he said. 'Most regrettably, it was smashed on the journey home. The box proved to be insufficiently strong to protect it. A great shame.'

I said no more and resumed the unpacking. I shared the Chaplain's distress. It was indeed a most unfortunate accident.

Christ Empowered Living

Selwyn Hughes

The human personality has been damaged by sin. So often we find ourselves searching for our self-worth and significance outside of God.

'Endless hours have been spent trying to help people understand and overcome those things that hinder the life of God within them spreading to all parts of their personalities...This book contains the spiritual rationale by which I have operated in helping people overcome their problems and move toward the kind of life where they exchange their own natural enthusiasm for Christ's abundant and inexhaustible resources – to experience Christ-empowered living.'

CWR
ISBN: 1-8534-5201-7

Price: 5.99

£3.99 with voucher

Published by CWR
Waverley Abbey House, Waverley Lane, Farnham,
Surrey, GU9 8EP

CHAPTER 11

STAYING ON COURSE

Billy Graham has often pointed out that it is not as a president but as a king that Christ wants to rule our lives. A president serves for a period of time and then goes out of office. A king rules for life. It is one thing to have Christ in our lives; it is another thing to let him reside permanently at the center.

Throughout time many people have professed to welcome Christ as King but then have sought to retain their own authority in certain areas of their lives. Then he is not King. "A truly kingly rule," I heard one preacher say, "is without limit, and it is that kind of rule he [Christ] asks us willingly to accept."

Jesus Christ wants to rule in us over the whole of our lives – home life, business life, social life, public life, and, of course, the inner life. He is not willing to be shut out from even one part of our personalities.

Only as Christ and his principles are allowed to hold sway in every part of our lives can he empower us to live the life he designed for us. Surely this makes sense. If Jesus Christ is to empower us to live life the way it should be lived, then he cannot consent to be excluded from any territory that Satan could use.

Steven Covey, in *The Seven Habits of Highly Effective People,* likens the course of our lives to that of an airplane as it flies from one destination to another. Before the plane takes off, the pilots have a clear flight plan. They know where they are going, but during the course of the flight, wind, rain, turbulence, air traffic, human error, and other factors act upon the plane, causing slight deviations to the flight plan. But barring extreme weather systems or the need to divert, planes usually arrive safely at their destination. This is because during the flight the pilots receive constant feedback from control towers, other airplanes, even the stars, which enable them to keep returning to the flight plan.

How can we stay on course in our Christian lives, dealing with all of life's issues in a way that reveals the inevitable consequences of Christ living within? That is the focus of the next two chapters.

This does not mean that we will never encounter problems, but it will help us cope with them and turn the stumbling blocks into stepping-stones.

Human beings, we remind ourselves, are made up of four areas of functioning: we can relate, think, choose, feel, all within a physical frame. But while we can *think* of the various parts of human functioning separately, they are never separate in experience. At different times, different parts of our being may be uppermost, but all are always present. The most logical of persons is not always thinking. The most ardent lover is not always feeling. All parts of our being intermingle, and there is a constant interaction among them.

So what steps do we need to maintain spiritual health and ensure that our personalities function in the way they were designed?

THE STARTING POINT

We must begin by thinking about the physical. Why make the starting point the physical and not the spiritual? Because when anything goes wrong in this part of our beings, it can have a direct influence on our thoughts and our moods. It follows that we ought, as far as possible, to do as much as we can to take care of the physical.

Several verses of Scripture might help bring this into focus:

> *He who does not use his endeavours to heal himself is brother to him who commits suicide.*
>
> (Prov. 18:9 Amplified Version)

> *It is God's will that ... each of you should learn to control his own body in a way that is holy and honorable.*
>
> (1 Thess. 4:3–4)

> *I do not run like a man running aimlessly; I do not fight like a man beating the air. No, I beat my body and make it my slave so that after I have preached to others, I myself will not be disqualified for the prize.*
>
> (1 Cor. 9:26–27)

We made the point earlier that through the medium of the body, the health of the spirit is shown. The body is presented by the spirit, and through this devotion of the body, the spirit expresses itself in worship. Perhaps much of what we think is worship is negated when we violate the temple in which God dwells – when we abuse the body by overwork, stress, and other things.

Some sicknesses we are powerless to do anything about, but as I heard one medical doctor say, "A Christian has no right to be sicker than he or she ought to be." We must commit ourselves, as far as we possibly can, to be good tenants of the Lord's property.

This is what C. S. Lewis said regarding the body in his *Letters to Malcolm: Chiefly on Prayer.*

> Mine has led me into many scrapes, but I've led it into far more. If the imagination were obedient the appetites would give us very little trouble. And from how much has it saved me! But for our body one whole realm of God's glory – all that we receive through the senses – would go unpraised. For the beasts can't appreciate it and the angels are, I suppose, pure intelligence. They understand colors and tastes better than our greatest scientists, but have they retinas or palates? I fancy the "beauties of nature" are a secret God has shared with us alone.

In the early years of my pastoral life, a church member had some strange views about his physical being. He told me that he despised his body, and when I questioned him over this, he said, "Yes, I hate my body, and it is quite biblical to do so. The physical part of us is vile and should be rejected. The apostle Paul despised his body, and so should we."

When I asked for a scriptural basis for his argument, he read me Paul's words in Philippians 3:21 in the King James Version. The KJV uses the phrase: "our vile body." I pointed out to him that the word translated *vile* in the King James Version means "lowly" and that Paul was saying our present bodies – subject as they are to weakness – are indeed "lowly" compared to the higher and incorruptible bodies we shall be given in the resurrection.

To treat one's body with disrespect is to disrespect God. If the truth is faced, we treat our cars with more respect than our bodies. In his book *The Way to Power and Praise*, E. Stanley Jones, under the title "What Would the Body Say?" wrote:

> I have sometimes imagined a convention of bodies met to discuss their inhabitants. One body stands up and says: "I wish the man that occupies me knew how to live. He doesn't so I'm tied in knots half the time." Another body stands up and says: "The woman who inhabits me is afraid to live. She's always inventing ways to escape living. She drinks and smokes, hoping that will let her out. But each time I protest by a reaction into dullness and lethargy, she whips me up again. But it's all a losing game, and some day I'm going to quit protesting and I'm going to give up and die." It's too bad that these humans don't know how to live.
>
> Another body stands up and says: "Look at my condition. I'm all black and blue inside – and I'm showing it on the outside too. The person who lives in me has taken to being resentful toward life and has a chronic grouch. You should see how my gastric juices refuse to flow under these conditions. And now this silly person is dosing himself with medicines and running from doctor to doctor, who can't find a thing wrong with me. I know what is wrong: I don't work very well with resentments. I like good will."

Literalists might object to this and say our bodies do not talk, but they do. They talk in the only language they know, the language of protest; and the protest shows itself through upset, disease, and pain.

Here are some suggestions I have used when counseling to help people keep their bodies in good repair.

Get a regular physical checkup and, if possible, by someone who understands the holistic approach. We are not just bodies but souls, and what happens in the soul is important. Those who function only at the physical level are lost. If you do not believe me, for I have had no medical training, then listen to what the physician John Sarno says in his book *Healing Back Pain*:

> I believe that all medical studies are flawed if they do not consider the emotional factor. For example, a research project dealing with the hardening of the arteries usually includes consideration of the diet (cholesterol), weight, exercise, genetic factors – but if it does not include emotional factors, the results in my view are not valid.

If physical weaknesses are discovered, consider how much may be caused by emotional functioning. Some problems are purely physical, though some believe that every physical problem is influenced in some way by the emotions. But be careful not to go to the other extreme – that all disease is mental and spiritual. That is grievous error.

Begin an exercise program. Our bodies were made to move, and we must keep them moving as much as possible. Control your weight. Watch what is happening. And don't be like the person who said, "Whenever I feel the need for exercise, I lie down until it goes away." People who don't or won't exercise have little willpower.

Consider also the importance of nutrition. Eating the right foods is a necessary part of keeping fit. In his book *Abundant Living*, E. Stanley Jones quotes James S. McLester:

> In the past, science has conferred on those people who have availed themselves of the newer knowledge of infectious diseases, better health and a greater average of life. In the future, it

promises to those races who will take advantage of the new knowledge of nutrition a larger stature, greater vigour, increased longevity and a higher level of cultural development.

Take vitamins. Jones also quotes Dr. L. R. Greene:

Life's chemical reactions are disturbed more frequently by a deficiency of vitamins than by any other cause. For instance a deficiency of Vitamin A gives rise to kidney, skin and gastrointestinal disorders, diarrhoea, poor appetite, bad teeth, chronic colitis, bronchitis, malnutrition followed by a greatly lowered state of general health and a high death rate from infectious diseases.

Watch what you eat. More than a millennium ago Hippocrates wrote: "Let your food be your medicine." Diet and nutrition are important. And watch your weight.

And, of course, consider that God heals. Some powerful words in the Epistle of James are astonishingly ignored by some churches:

Is any one of you sick? He should call the elders of the church to pray over him and anoint him with oil in the name of the Lord. And the prayer offered in faith will make the sick person well; the Lord will raise him up. If he has sinned, he will be forgiven. Therefore confess your sins to each other and pray for each other so that you may be healed.

(James 5:14–16)

If your church doesn't practise that biblical injunction, then go to one that does. God heals today. I can tell you that I wouldn't be here today unless that were true.

UNDERSTAND YOUR LONGINGS

The truth that God made us as longing beings is one that has been strongly emphasized throughout this book. Deep in the heart of every one of us, we have been saying there are longings for relationship – first with the living God and then with other thinking, feeling, choosing beings like ourselves.

Because we are made in the image of God, everyone – even the most hardened atheist – reaches out to him. They would not admit to this, of course, but as G. K. Chesterton said: "When a man knocks at the door of a brothel, he is really looking for God."

An atheist once said to me: "I don't believe in God, but I would like to, if only to satisfy the desire that seems to be within me for transcendence."

Understanding that we are longing beings and how to deal with those longings is crucial to keeping our lives on course spiritually. Permit me to lay down a few propositions to help you do that.

First, fix in your mind that you have longings within you that nothing on earth can satisfy. Multitudes have said if they only had this or that, they would always be happy. Some have died believing it. The evidence shows, however, that when they obtained what they believed would bring them happiness, they found that it satisfied for only a little while, and then there was the old persistent thirst back again, clamorous and as demanding as ever.

Alister McGrath in *Bridge Building* tells the story of Boris Becker, the noted tennis player who came close to taking his own life while overwhelmed with a sense of hopelessness and emptiness. Even though he was a tremendously successful tennis champion, he felt something was wrong:

I had won Wimbledon twice before, once as the youngest player. I was rich. I had all the material possessions I needed: money, cars, women, everything ... I know that this is a cliché. It's the old song of the movie and pop stars who commit suicide. They have everything and yet they are unhappy ... I had no inner peace. I was a puppet on a string.

Some believe money will satisfy the ache that lies at the core of the human spirit. And some set their mind on a coveted position and believe obtaining it will bring them complete satisfaction. Fame – what Milton called "the last infirmity of noble minds" – is what appeals to others.

Still others seek pleasure, believing that will satisfy the ache in their soul. Lord Byron, whom one biographer described as "typical of the grosser hedonist," drifted in his search for pleasure from one woman to another and died an old man at the age of thirty-six. He said of himself on his last birthday:

My days are in the yellow leaf;
    The flowers and fruits of love are gone;
The worm, the canker, and the grief
    Are mine alone!

There are those also who believe that perfect physical health is what brings satisfaction. In our own day and generation, fitness has become almost a cult; but these who worship at its shrine fail to realize there are spiritual ills no harmony of the body can cure and, if they remain uncured, will rob the body of its health as well. That is the first fact: there is something in all of us that the best things on earth – husbands, wives, friends, or health – cannot satisfy.

ACKNOWLEDGE YOUR LONGINGS

Here is a second truth: Only as you acknowledge your longings will you be able to move beyond them. Not to acknowledge unfulfilled longings is to be driven to search for satisfaction in other ways. One of the saddest things to behold is a Christian who remains content with practicing the duties of the Christian life and relying on them to bring satisfaction rather than engaging in a dynamic and passionate relationship with God.

John Eldridge's statement bears quoting again at this juncture: "If Christianity does not take our breath away, then something else will." We will redouble our efforts in other directions (sometimes spiritual ones) to compensate for the lack of aliveness we feel in our souls.

A. W. Tozer said, "Thirsty hearts are those whose longings have been awakened by the touch of God within them." Listen to your heart. In *The Sacred Romance*, authors Brent Curtis and John Eldridge make this point most forcefully:

> Aren't you thirsty? Listen to your heart … We join a small group and read a book on establishing a more effective prayer life. We train to be part of a church evangelism team. We tell ourselves that the malaise of spirit we feel even as we step up our religious activity is a sign of spiritual immaturity and we scold our heart for its lack of fervour … The voice in our heart dares to speak to us again. Listen to me, there is something missing in all this. You long to be in a love affair, an adventure. You were made for something more. You know it.

The love affair and the adventure that these writers talk about can never be found in service for Christ, but in

Christ and Christ alone. Do not misunderstand me: Our service for him is important, but the most important issue in the Christian life is not what we do for him but what he does for us. The deepest longings of our heart cannot be met except in a personal relationship with Jesus Christ.

Take this incident recorded in John's Gospel:

> *On the last and greatest day of the Feast, Jesus stood and said in a loud voice, "If anyone is thirsty, let him come to me and drink. Whoever believes in me, as the Scripture has said, streams of living water will flow from within him."*

> (John 7:37–38)

The feast referred to here was the Feast of Tabernacles (2 Chron. 8:13; Ezra 3:4; Zech. 14:16), also called the feast of ingathering (Exod. 23:16; 34:22), and celebrated the dwelling in booths (or tabernacles), which were to be joyful reminders to Israel (Lev. 23:41; Deut. 16:14) of God's provision for them in the wilderness. It lasted for seven days (Lev. 23:36; Deut. 16:13; Ezek. 45:25), and on the eighth day they had a "closing assembly" when every Israelite lived in booths in commemoration of the fact that their fathers lived this way after their exodus from Egypt. Josephus referred to this feast as the holiest and greatest of the Hebrew feasts.

On the last day of the feast, the priest would go down to the pool of Siloam, draw water from it, then return to the temple precincts and pour it into the dry earth, once again commemorating God's provision of water for his ancient people when they traveled through the wilderness.

Now against that background consider once again the words of John: "If anyone is thirsty, let him come to me and drink" (John 7:37). Note that when he uttered those words, they were said not in measured tones but in a "loud voice." It was not often that Jesus shouted. I imagine that more often than not he spoke in calm, measured tones. But on this occasion something moved his soul so deeply that he stood (in those days teachers usually sat) and shouted.

What was it that stirred our Lord so much that made him stand up and cry out? Perhaps this: As the Savior witnessed the pageantry and ceremony going on around him and sensing that both people and priests were depending on the religious ritual rather than a personal relationship with the living God to satisfy their spiritual thirst, he was moved to shout out in their midst, "Come to me and drink."

His voice still rings out across the centuries with the same message: Come to me, he says, not to your wife, husband, friend, or any other thing. I am the only One who can slake your thirst. Come to me and drink.

That is the second fact: If we do not acknowledge our deep longings for God, we will remain satisfied with duty rather than devotion, with the things of Christ rather than with Christ himself.

PEOPLE OF PASSION

The third truth is this: The only satisfying relationship with God is a passionate one. Several years ago, on the verge of retiring from active counseling, I sat down and began to think if a common denominator had been evident in the lives of the Christians who had sat in my counseling room asking for spiritual help. It did not take me long to conclude that one thing stood out above all others – lack of spiritual passion.

Many of these people were good Christians in many ways. They attended church, read their Bibles regularly, prayed, took care of their families, and saw themselves as dutiful Christians, but they appeared to have so little passion in their lives.

Some were ministers who saw themselves more as performers than desperately thirsty servants needing to drink daily from "the spring of living water" (Jer. 2:13). I tell you again – with all the force and conviction of which I am capable – if we do not have a close and intimate relationship with God through his Son, Jesus Christ, no matter how dutiful we may be in observing the rules of Christian living, we will have little spiritual passion in our lives.

Whenever I peruse the words of the apostles John, Peter, and Paul in the New Testament, I sense the passion for God that flowed through their hearts. Take the apostle John's words in the Revelation:

> *To him who loves us and has freed us from our sins by his blood, and has made us to be a kingdom and priests to serve his God and Father – to him be glory and power for ever and ever! Amen.*

(Rev. 1:5–6)

The words in our English translations do not bring out the flavor of the Greek. In the original language the words come across as a burst of impassioned thankfulness.

I can never read these words of John without thinking of a little poem quoted by Ian Macpherson in *This Man Loveth Me.* Poet W. S. Landor talks about a man who is near to dying and reflects on how his wife of just a few years will deal with his death. He pictures her coming to his graveside, paying her respects, and then quickly moving on to other things:

Proud word you never spoke, but you will speak .
    For not exempt from pride some future day
Resting on one white hand a warm wet cheek
    Over my open volume you will say
This man loved me, then rise and trip away.

John seems to be saying the same thing: "This man loved me," he cries in effect. But he cannot rise and trip away. He must go on to worship.

The apostle Peter also speaks with passion in several sections of his epistles. Take this verse for example:

> *Praise be to the God and Father of our Lord Jesus Christ! In his great mercy he has given us new birth into a living hope through the resurrection of Jesus Christ from the dead, and into an inheritance that can never perish, spoil or fade – kept in heaven for you, who through faith are shielded by God's power until the coming of the salvation that is ready to be revealed in the last time.*

(1 Pet. 1:3–5)

As he talks about God's great overflowing mercy vouchsafed to us in Christ, can you not sense the joy bubbling up within his soul? Peter was not just a dutiful follower of the Master. He was one of his impassioned disciples. Praise and gratitude overflow from him simply because they must.

Paul was a man of passion also. Whenever I read his letter to the Romans, I am intrigued when I read that after dealing with the most taxing theology, his heart overflows in gratitude to God. Theology turns to doxology as he contemplates all that God has done for us in Christ. Listen to him as he pauses for a moment to allow the feelings in his soul to find expression:

> *Oh, the depth of the riches of the wisdom and knowledge of God! How*
> *unsearchable his judgments, and his paths beyond tracing out! "Who*
> *has known the mind of the Lord? Or who has been his counselor?"*
> *"Who has ever given to God, that God should repay him?"*
>
> (Rom. 11:32–35)

These New Testament writers were head over heels in love
with Jesus Christ. Their pens seem to catch fire as they tell
how his passion fired their passion. That is the third fact:
Nothing will satisfy our soul like a passionate relationship
with Jesus Christ.

TUNE IN TO YOUR LONGINGS

My next point is this: Tune in to your longings. This
means more than just acknowledging them. It means
getting in touch with the fact that you are a thirsty, longing being. Focus on that fact and feel that thirst. Our
desire to know God and enjoy him depends on how
aware we are of what we lack. The more deeply we feel
our thirst, the more deeply we will drink of Christ and
the more eagerly we will be drawn to the source of true
satisfaction. So tune in to the deep thirsts and the deep
longings within your soul. If you are not willing to feel
the deep longings that God has placed within you for
himself, you will live on the surface of life and come to
believe that anything can satisfy it.

The words of Simone Weil, in her book *Waithing for*
God, are pertinent and powerful:

> The danger is not lest the soul should doubt whether there is
> any bread, but lest by a lie, it should persuade itself that it is not

hungry. It can only persuade itself of this by lying, for the reality of its hunger is not a belief but a certainty.

Whenever I have made this point to people in the past – to tune in to your deep longings – the first question they ask is, but how?

I suggest this: Take a sheet of paper and think of the times you have been disappointed in your life. Focus on how many times you have longed for someone to come through for you but they let you down. What were you longing for that was not met? How hurt were you in those moments? Was it because you depended too much on others to give you what your soul longed for?

Imagine, too, how you would handle such things as criticism, rejection, or disappointment if you were fully aware of how much you were loved by God. Was not the reason you were hurt so much because you looked to others and depended on them to meet the needs of your soul that only God can meet?

Does this mean that when we learn to rely on God for the security, significance, and worth that we no longer experience disappointment or need the love of others? No. We will still hurt, still be disappointed, and still desire the affection and affirmation of others; but if and when it is not there – providing our relationship with God is intact – we can still go on; we can still function.

People may hurt us and let us down, but they cannot destroy us. Our engagement with a living God does not insulate us from feelings of hurt or make us invulnerable to disappointment, but it does uphold us so that we can go on loving others as our own souls are loved.

A word of caution: Tuning in to your deep longings must not become an obsessive exercise. I would describe it as something to be glanced at rather than to be gazed at. And be aware that tuning in to your longings will cause some uncomfortable feelings to rise within you. One such feeling will be that of helplessness. We saw earlier that the soul, because of the damage sin has caused, abhors the feeling of helplessness. Our carnal nature likes to feel it is in control, that it can meet the soul's demands through self-effort. It can't, but it likes to feel it can. Nothing is more humbling than a recognition of a thirst that only God can quench.

Another uncomfortable feeling that will arise is a sense of dependency. It is uncomfortable because God has made us dependent beings, but sin reverses that and works to make us feel independent. The soul, because of its fallen condition, hates to feel dependent; and yielding control for our soul's function to God is not easy. But it must be done.

It is not easy to face the fact that we are longing beings. To get in touch with the thirst in our souls means that things like helplessness and the sense of dependency surface and bring with them a challenge. This is why many people deny their longings and pretend they are not there. But denial exposes us all the more powerfully to their unnoticed tyranny.

My point is this: Trust God to meet your deepest longings. Turn from dependency on other things to dependence on him. *Trust*, as we saw, is another word for *faith*. Sin is antitrust. I have met many people in the Christian life who can trust God with things like finance, healing, and choice of a career but are unable to trust him with their longings.

Here's a challenge we must face. Can we trust God to meet the deepest longings of our hearts, the longings for security, self-worth, and significance, or do we turn to other things? To live a life of dependency on God means that we come before him in absolute dependency, believing that if he doesn't come through for us, then we are sunk.

CHASING GOD

My final point is this: Learn to pant after God as did the psalmist. Take this brief selection of statements from the Psalms:

> *As the deer pants for streams of water, so my soul pants for you, O God. My soul thirsts for God, for the living God. When can I go and meet with God?*
>
> (Ps. 42:1–2)

> *I spread out my hands to you; my soul thirsts for you like a parched land.*
>
> (Ps. 143:6)

> *O God, you are my God, earnestly I seek you; my soul thirsts for you, my body longs for you, in a dry and weary land where there is no water.*
>
> (Ps. 63:1)

Some time ago I read the comments of Paul Weaver, who briefly reviewed a book called *The God Chasers* by Tommy Tenney. He said: "I found the title particularly intriguing. After all, how can you chase God? I started reading the book and could not put it down. It challenged my life and whetted my appetite for more of God. *There is so much about God that I know so little about.*"

What does it mean to chase after God? Or as the psalmist put it, to pant after him? It means several things. It means realizing there is so much about God that I know so little about. The apostle Paul, a man who knew more about God than most, cries out in his epistle to the Philippians:

> *I want to know Christ and the power of his resurrection and the fellowship of sharing in his sufferings, becoming like him in his death.*
>
> (Phil. 3:10)

Someone has said, "The beginning of education is the realization of your ignorance." It is the same in the spiritual life. The beginning of spiritual development is the realization of how little of God we know. Consider that, and let it whet your appetite to know more of him.

Another thing that "panting after God" means is to make him the soul's central focus. This means much more than attending church on Sunday, making sure you say your prayers before you go to sleep, or occasionally reading a brief portion from the Scriptures. The pursuit of the soul after God calls for discipline and determination.

It means lingering before him in prayer, feeding your soul as much as you can on his Word, meditating in that Word, and as a friend of mine puts it, "letting your soul loose to find its home in God." The New King James Version translates Psalm 63:8 this way: "My soul follows close behind You." He could well have said, "My soul chases after God."

A third thing that panting after God means is knowing him for who he is, not just what he gives. Tommy Tenney says in his book that God Chasers are people who are more interested in the face of God than his hands. Christians, he

claims, are so consumer-oriented that they are more interested in getting something from God than in knowing him
for who he is. God's purpose is for us to know him
intimately, to gaze upon his face, knowing that as we do,
our soul will find him to be its delight.

Ask yourself: "How deeply do I long after God? To
what lengths am I prepared to go in order to know him
better?" The soul is capable of great passion; we see this in
great music and great art. The truth is that none of us have
been able to find in our relationships more than just a taste
of what we long for. We were designed to be drawn, to pant
after God. "But why is it necessary to acknowledge our
deep longings and our deep thirst?" Because only thirsty
people drink.

Keep ever before you, therefore, the thought that you
are a longing being, with longings that only God can satisfy.
If this constant awareness is not in your soul, then you will
seek your satisfaction elsewhere. Let there be no doubt
whatsoever about that.

It means lingering before him in prayer, feeding your
soul as much as you can on his Word, meditating in that
Word, and as a friend of mine puts it, "letting your soul
loose to find its home in God." The New King James
Version translates Psalm 63:8 this way: "My soul follows
close behind You." He could well have said, "My soul
chases after God."

A third thing that panting after God means is knowing
him for who he is, not just what he gives. Tommy Tenney
says in his book that God Chasers are people who are more
interested in the face of God than his hands. Christians, he
claims, are so consumer-oriented that they are more interested in getting something from God than in knowing him
for who he is. God's purpose is for us to know him

intimately, to gaze upon his face, knowing that as we do, our soul will find him to be its delight.

Ask yourself: "How deeply do I long after God? To what lengths am I prepared to go in order to know him better?" The soul is capable of great passion; we see this in great music and great art. The truth is that none of us have been able to find in our relationships more than just a taste of what we long for. We were designed to be drawn, to pant after God. "But why is it necessary to acknowledge our deep longings and our deep thirst?" Because only thirsty people drink.

Keep ever before you, therefore, the thought that you are a longing being, with longings that only God can satisfy. If this constant awareness is not in your soul, then you will seek your satisfaction elsewhere. Let there be no doubt whatsoever about that.

It means lingering before him in prayer, feeding your soul as much as you can on his Word, meditating in that Word, and as a friend of mine puts it, "letting your soul loose to find its home in God." The New King James Version translates Psalm 63:8 this way: "My soul follows close behind You." He could well have said, "My soul chases after God."

A third thing that panting after God means is knowing him for who he is, not just what he gives. Tommy Tenney says in his book that God Chasers are people who are more interested in the face of God than his hands. Christians, he claims, are so consumer-oriented that they are more inter-ested in getting something from God than in knowing him for who he is. God's purpose is for us to know him inti-mately, to gaze upon his face, knowing that as we do, our soul will find him to be its delight.

Ask yourself: "How deeply do I long after God? To what lengths am I prepared to go in order to know him better?" The soul is capable of great passion; we see this in great music and great art. The truth is that none of us have been able to find in our relationships more than just a taste of what we long for. We were designed to be drawn, to pant after God. "But why is it necessary to acknowledge our deep longings and our deep thirst?" Because only thirsty people drink.

Keep ever before you, therefore, the thought that you are a longing being, with longings that only God can satisfy. If this constant awareness is not in your soul, then you will seek your satisfaction elsewhere. Let there be no doubt whatsoever about that.

Unlocking

Adrian Plass

'I am a frightened person. God began the unlocking process in me a long time ago, and it's still going on today. I'm sure that God wants to tackle the fears that cripple us…'

Come with Adrian Plass on a journey through the Bible, starting with the temptation of Jesus in the desert and ending with Mary in the garden on Resurrection morning. Along the way, discover some of the many ways in which God meets us right where we are, no matter what our circumstances, and how he helps us learn for ourselves the meaning of 'the truth will set you free'.

The Bible Reading Fellowship
ISBN: 0-7459-3510-9

Price: £6.99

£4.99 with voucher

Published by The Bible Reading Fellowship
First Floor, Elsfield Hall, 15-17 Elsfield Way,
Oxford, OX2 8EP

Introduction

I am a frightened person. God began the unlocking process in me a long time ago, and it's still going on today. I'm sure that God *wants* to tackle the fears that cripple us. The resurrection of Jesus made all things possible and the Holy Spirit moves in our lives with all the ingenuity of the Creator God. That doesn't actually make it any easier to identify methods or techniques. God has as many solutions as there are people with fears, and they're all going to be different.

So what can we do? What will different solutions have in common? What is God's plan for frightened people?

I think the first part of the answer is that members of the body of Christ need to learn to depend on each other much more than has been the case in the recent years of feverishly pursued individual spiritual achievement. You'll read a lot about that in this book.

Secondly, in every case I know of where fear has been overcome, an essential truth has become stronger than that fear. Jesus summed it up: 'Then you will know the truth, and the truth will set you free.'

That's it in a nutshell, but, as you know, some nutshells are very hard to crack. Let's have a go, though.

Each of the pieces you're about to read begins with a look at the truth as it's given to us by God in the Bible. I'll then respond to the passage as honestly as I can, hoping that as many readers as possible will identify with my ravings! (Do feel free to laugh or cry.) Then I'll invite you to join me in praying from the heart about the issues that have arisen. The book was originally written for Lent studies, and is arranged in sections, but please don't fall into the trap of thinking that you've got to stick to a particular one, or that you'll lose your salvation if you skip one of the pieces. Use the book in any way you want. My dearest wish is that, as you read, you'll forget about me, and just be close to this wonderful God of ours.

By the way, the other essential ingredient is obedience. if, after talking to him, he tells you to do something, for goodness' sake do it! Don't worry if it seems strange or 'not quite your style' – just do it!

God bless you as you join me now, and I pray from the bottom of my heart that something in this book will begin the process of releasing you from your fear. Let the unlocking begin.

Where we begin

The desert and the devil

Then Jesus was led by the Spirit into the desert to be tempted by the devil. After fasting for forty days and forty nights, he was hungry. The tempter came to him and said, 'If you are the Son of God, tell these stones to become bread.' Jesus answered, 'It is written: "Man does not live on bread alone, but on every word that comes from the mouth of God." ' Then the devil took him to the holy city and had him stand on the highest point of the temple. 'If you are the Son of God,' he said, 'throw yourself down. For it is written: "He will command his angels concerning you, and they will lift you up in their hands, so that you will not strike your foot against a stone." ' Jesus answered him, 'It is also written: "Do not put the Lord your God to the test." ' Again, the devil took him to a very high mountain and showed him all the kingdoms of the world and their splendour. 'All this I will give you,' he said, 'if you will bow down and worship me.' Jesus said to him, 'Away from me, Satan! For it is written: "Worship the Lord your God, and serve him only." ' Then the devil left him, and angels came and attended him.

Matthew 4:1–11

For those of us who value our salvation (and there are a few of us still roaming the Jurassic Park of Christendom) it is worth reflecting that during this period of forty days the whole salvation plan could have failed completely. Jesus was truly man, and therefore must have been capable of giving in to temptation. If this was not so, his ministry in general, and these forty days in particular, become a nonsense.

The Gospel accounts of this crucial event are fairly brief, and can't even begin to convey the agony of mind, body and spirit that Jesus must have endured as he wrestled with temptations to use selfishly the incredible power that now flooded through him. We can discard the mental picture of a tall, noble, clear-eyed, blond hero with a tame cherubim perched on his shoulder like a chubby parrot, dismissing Satan with an airy wave of the hand. After almost six weeks of fasting in the heat of the desert, reviewing again and again the fatal implications of total commitment to his Father, Jesus, thin and weary, must have come seriously close to adopting the way of the world and the devil. Material possessions, personal safety and ultimate power were set before him like a three-runged ladder to earthly contentment. In his weakened state it must have seemed a very attractive option compared to three years of celibacy, conflict and rejection, followed by one of the most painful forms of execution ever devised by man. Jesus didn't give jn to temptation. He flung scriptural truths at the devil, rather as David flung stones at Goliath. And the comparison is a fair one. Jesus had to win this battle as a real man supported by God, even though he was also God, so that it could be possible for him to say to ordinary men and women, 'Be perfect, even as I am perfect.' It is a mystery beyond mysteries, but, like many mysteries, it quite easily finds a home in the secret heart of our understanding.

There is a profound fear in many Christians that they will fail in their own wilderness experience. At one time or another each of us is asked to walk into the desert and face the question about where our final commitment lies. It feels awfully dark to give away the world and all that it might offer, but it is the beginning of ministry. Jesus was armed with knowledge of the Scriptures, and (as long as we don't get silly about it) so should we be. He also walked *voluntarily* into that desert. God doesn't push people into the wilderness, but if we find ourselves there he might well suggest that the time has come to make the most basic choice of all.

Have I made that choice? Well, I've certainly been in a desert or two, and I've seen the options lined up before me quite clearly. I've tried to dismiss the devil, with only partial success, but opportunities are still graciously offered to me by God, and Jesus died to bridge the gap between what I am and what I should be, so I remain optimistic.

The thing I'm really looking forward to, if I ever do finally resist Satan, is the bit where the angels appear with a bottle of lemonade and a packet of sandwiches.

Pray with me

Father, deserts are not nice places, but we need them because the rich and verdant places are so distracting. Part of us really wants to resist the devil and commit ourselves to you, but we are afraid. The world is so much with us. it seems ,safe and familiar and far more attractive than a risky walk with you. Thank you for Jesus who felt all these things, but fought his way through to victory for you and for us. As we follow your Son across the wilderness of our own fears, help us to be strong in you and resistant to the voice of Satan, who wants us to believe that nothing ever really changes for the better. Amen.

The way we were

> 'I tell you, whoever acknowledges me before men, the Son of Man will also acknowledge him before the angels of God. But he who disowns me before men will be disowned before the angels of God.'
>
> Luke 12:8–9

When I first became a Christian at the age of sixteen I did some ridiculous things. Once, at a Christian youth club a few miles from my home, I literally bullied some poor, mild non-Christian into a back room and on to his knees, so that he could make a commitment using a prayer dictated by my good self. I can still see his wild, staring eyes as he was pitchforked into the Kingdom by a tall, skinny (yes, I said skinny) fanatic who wasn't going to take 'No' for an answer. If, by some miracle of God's grace, that fellow is a Christian today, and he's reading this – I do apologize. I wouldn't do that today.

Customers in the coffee-drinking dens of Tunbridge Wells must have got pretty fed up with me too. Armed with my regulation-issue Bible and burning enthusiasm, I would harangue anyone and everyone about the need to 'get right with God'. Sensitivity didn't come into it. I told them about Jesus whether they wanted to hear or not. Of course, I wouldn't do it like that now.

Later, when I was eighteen or nineteen, I went off to theatre school in Bristol, accompanied by the same Bible and the same attitude. I clutched that Bible to me like Linus clutches his blanket. Poor old Bristolians. The scruffy evangelist was among them, still cornering people in bars and cafés and on public transport, and enquiring about the state of their souls. Naturally, I would approach it all very differently today.

Later still, I found myself working with children who had educational problems, at a boarding school in Gloucestershire. My zeal had abated a little, but I almost didn't get the job because I said I was a 'born-again Christian' on the application form.

One day, I was playing cricket with one of the boys in a practice net at the edge of the field. He hit the ball out of the net and into some bushes. We looked for ages, but with no luck. Finally, I said to him, 'We'll pray about it, shall we?'

'Eh?' said the boy.

'I'll ask God to find the ball for us.'

'Eh?

'Father, we know you're interested in little things, so will you please help us to find our ball?'

When I opened my eyes I looked down and saw that the ball was lying on the ground between the boy's feet. His eyes nearly fell out of his head. I was really pleased to see the ball, but, of course, I wouldn't approach a similar situation in that naïve way nowadays.

Last week, I was trying to get a car boot open for a friend. We tugged and fiddled and prised and pulled and pushed, but nothing made any difference. As I knelt at the back of the car, clean out of options, it occurred to me that I could ask God to help us. I did ask him silently but something told me that only an 'out-loud' prayer was going to he any use here. I chickened out. I publicly acknowledge Jesus all the time, but I'm a bit out of practice when it comes to the private sector.

I did do a lot of very silly things when I was a young Christian, and I'm sure a lot of people found me a real pain in the neck, but I feel sad when I compare my readiness to tell everybody that my life belonged to Jesus, and that theirs ought to as well, with the way I speak to people now

I think I've got a bit frightened of being simple about my
faith in ordinary situations, and, now that I've read this
passage again, I think I ought to do something about it.

Pray with me

> *Father, I feel a bit of a fool when I look back at those early years, but*
> *there was a sort of childlike passion in me then that just overflowed all*
> *the time. I certainly don't want to be that particular kind of idiot again,*
> *but I wouldn't mind being a different kind of idiot now. I want to be*
> *ready to acknowledge you openly and enthusiastically at the right time,*
> *and to he sensitive enough to know when it's the wrong time. It's ridic-*
> *ulous that I should he frightened of using your Son's name after all*
> *these years. Perhaps I need to fall in love with him all over again.*
> *Grant me a fresh vision of your love, Lord, a new excitement that can't*
> *help communicating itself to others. Thank you. Amen.*

Behind the Songs

Graham Kendrick

At the age of 15 Graham Kendrick announced to his parents his dream: to be a songwriter. Within just a few years he was travelling the country performing his trademark acoustic story-songs and recording albums.

Since that time his songs have become the soundtrack for the spiritual journeys of countless people and his praise and worship compositions are regularly on the lips of millions around the world.

Through the window of his lyrics, the famous alongside the lesser-known, Graham takes us behind the songs into the inspiration and circumstances which brought them into being. There are fascinating insights into the man himself, and thought-provoking reflections on the genre he helped create.

Kevin Mayhew
ISBN:1–84003–735–0

Price:£12.99

£7.99 with voucher

First published in 2001 by Kevin Mayhew
Buxhall, Stowmarket, Suffolk, IP14 3DJ

Introduction

Graham Kendrick's songwriting has been part of the soundtrack for much of my Christian life. Whatever I was going through, his compositions were usually somewhere in the background – comforting me, challenging me, reminding me to keep the main thing, the main thing.

I first came across his music as a teenager while living in the north-west of England. My schoolmates were into Pink Floyd and Deep Purple. I was into Paul Simon and Ralph McTell! A friend at church said I ought to listen to this Christian singer called Graham Kendrick. It fitted the bill exactly: contemporary folk-rock with a sharp lyrical edge and honest, human poetry. 'The executioner' was a favourite, with its depth and drama.

There was a gig at Liverpool University where Graham played 'Make it soon', his song about the Second Coming. It had a deep impact on me, and on a few of my friends. We were on the leadership team of a big youth group at the time, and felt convicted about our corporate spiritual state. So we went forward for prayer. It was a powerful moment.

I remember one early Greenbelt. They called it a mudbath. The whole place got rained out. The main stage was abandoned. All the bands and artists had to set up their gear in a marquee. My mates and I managed to squeeze in near the front. Graham was on the bill that night. I remember him singing his 'signature tune' 'How much do you think you are worth?' It was a great atmosphere.

Years later, I was leading worship at a church on the south coast of England. Of course, Graham appeared again – we used several of his worship songs each week in the congregation When I joined one of the early March for Jesus events in London, once again we were Singing his material as we prayed at key 'powerbases'

When I finally met him at a March for Jesus celebration in Hyde Park, I plucked up the courage to tell him how much his music had meant to me. Instantly Graham changed from the confident international worship leader to a shy, sheepish bloke who didn't know how to respond to a compliment. That's what so many of us like about him.

This personal collection of Songs and memories is not just Graham's story. For everyone who's laughed, cried and stood in awe at what God has done across the Church Over the past 30 years, it's your story and it's my story

God bless you, Graham It's been a privilege working with you on this family album.

Clive Price

May 2001

Clive Price is a freelance journalist working with a number of Christian organisations and periodicals in Britain and the USA.

He is editor of Worship Together *magazine, UK correspondent for* Charisma *magazine, author of* Glorious Awakenings *(SPCK/Triangie), and co-author of the award-winning* Miracle Children *(Hodder & Stoughton).*

Married with three children, Clive lives in West Sussex.

Shine, Jesus, shine

Shine, Jesus, shine,
fill this land with the Father's glory;
blaze, Spirit, blaze,
set our hearts on fire.
Flow, river, flow,
flood the nations with grace and mercy;
send forth your word, Lord,
and let there be light.

Lord, the light of your love is shining,
in the midst of the darkness, shining;
Jesus, Light of the World, shine upon us,
set us free by the truth you now bring us,
shine on me, shine on me.

Lord, I come to your awesome presence,
from the shadows into your radiance;
by the blood I may enter your brightness,
search me, try me, consume all my darkness,
shine on me, shine on me.

As we gaze on your kingly brightness,
so our faces display your likeness,
ever changing from glory to glory,
mirrored here may our lives tell your story,
shine on me, shine on me.

Even the Pope has swung his cane in time to the music!

It was sung at the Dunblane memorial service. It's been used at Billy Graham crusades. It became one of the 'folk songs' of Spring Harvest lore. It has remained at the top end of the Church Copyright Licence charts for a decade, and become a standard in schools across the land. Even the Pope has swung his cane in time to the music! 'Shine, Jesus, shine' is one of those songs that just seemed to catch a moment when people were beginning to believe once again that a spiritual impact could be made on an entire nation.

At the time of writing it, Ichthus Christian Fellowship was focusing on the theme of the presence and holiness of God – the God who dwells in unapproachable light. I remember writing the three verses without the chorus and road-testing them. For some reason they weren't quite happening, so the song went back in the file for several months. Later, I came back to a phase of song-writing and I pulled it out again. I quickly concluded that actually this was not a complete song. All it had was three verses – and it needed a chorus.

The phrase 'Shine, Jesus, shine' came to mind. I think it was one of the quickest things I've ever written! Within 20 minutes or half-an-hour I'd written the chorus and the whole thing just needed a little bit of editing and tidying up here and there. The chorus fell into place surprisingly naturally. But even then it took a while to mature. I'd written the verses at a different pace. So the tempo of verse and chorus seemed to pull against one another. It was only through use that it actually began to settle down. As I worked on it with my band, an arrangement and a way of doing it took shape. Then it started to feel like a complete song.

It was used at Spring Harvest when it was still very new. And I still had no idea at all of its potential success. I'd written a whole batch of material during that time, and there were other songs that I preferred at the time which are now long forgotten.

I can remember singing it at Spring Harvest, where it became clear that much of the song's dynamics were in the content of that chorus. It's a prayer for the nation. Obviously I'd thought about it – I had the UK in my mind while I was singing it. But because it says 'fill this land', it's generic.

So then I started meeting people from other nations who were saying, 'This is like our national anthem'. Whenever they sang it, they sang it for their own country. I was so glad that I hadn't referred to Britain or England specifically.

It was one of those cases where people were beginning to catch a vision for God doing something on a national level. For my generation, such a wide-spread spiritual impact had almost seemed too big to contemplate. Decades of decline in the Church had produced a siege mentality, and it had become quite hard to imagine the nation being touched by the gospel. But faith was rising towards that, and the song was carried on a wave of prayer.

'Shine, Jesus, shine' was new and it caught the spirit of the moment. It was very Jesus-focused. Sometimes when I'm writing songs I ask the question of God, 'Can you endorse this song? Is there any reason why you can't put your stamp on it? Is there something about it that fails to expound the truth, exalt Jesus or offer an emphasis on something important?'

I am always painfully conscious of compositional or lyrical shortcomings in a song – especially if I see them only when it's too late for changes. But I am also aware of how gracious God is to take hold of these faulty vessels and use them, and it's often the case that in the singing of a song, the Spirit of God turns up in a special way. Someone told me about a church in Australia that had become very dry. Very little was happening. But they picked up on 'Shine, Jesus, shine' in its early days. The more they sang it, the more the Spirit of God started to move. I'm sure there were other factors involved, but the story goes that the song brought something new to them. At the very least it seemed that God turned up just when they were singing it!

I find that fascinating. It's something you always want to happen but it's something you can't possibly manufacture. It's something God decides to do. I often wish that I had the knowledge to look into how music presses certain buttons in the heart and mind. But because I've only ever been a play-it-by-ear musician, I've always worked intuitively.

Obviously there is some experience and wisdom that I've picked up along the way in terms of what makes a song work. But at its heart, I guess it's just me trying to do the best that I can and trusting that God is helping me and following it through until I have a complete song.

A key part of my road testing is to submit songs to friends at Ichthus. Faith Forster has been a particularly helpful editor of songs. She and others often point out things that could be a bit clearer, or they help me when I'm stuck and don't know where to take it conceptually. All these things contribute to the songwriting process.

Had I been trying to operate as an isolated individual, a great deal of this just wouldn't have happened. So I've been in a good place. That's not unusual. Many worship writers are based in a movement or church that has a very definite direction, and all the checks and balances are in place to protect, preserve and provoke them. All those elements are vital.

Ichthus was pioneering the praise marches before I ever came on board. When I started working with them, I was just giving expression to something they'd already put into place. I was offering my gifts to serve them in that context, to use music to give it more form and structure. Almost inadvertently I created a kind of liturgy for the streets. Suddenly other churches thought, 'Oh well, we know how to do it now – here's the simple key, we'll just use that.' It worked and they did it. The local church context has been of absolute importance.

It must be every songwriter's dream to see their material enjoy a broad connection with huge crowds of people. But there are other dynamics at work when a congregation embraces a particular song: the vocabulary has to sit well in people's mouths; if they feel uncomfortable singing it, it won't work; it can't be so personal to the writer that people can't sing it honestly and identify with it; the melody has to be accessible.

Strange as it may seem, it has probably helped that I don't have an amazingly versatile voice. It tends to take me to solid melodies within a fairly limited range. The chances are that if I'm comfortable singing it, then most people will be comfortable singing it, too.

I've always had a natural attraction to anthems. That might be my background in the hymns. It's been there for as long as I can remember, and that's obviously a great help.

I don't have any formal musical training and often envy people who do. I've learned mainly by trial and error. I take the 'hit and miss, try it this way, try it that way, hope for happy accidents' approach. It's probably not the most efficient way of writing songs! But now and again it works. The bottom line is if the song brings a release in my own spirit, perhaps it will produce that in other people, too.

I've had to learn to trust my instincts – and God's prompting. I have to trust that in the process God is helping me to write what will enable other people to worship. I'm not one to claim that a song was given to me straight from heaven. I actually think it's a wonder that God works with us rather than using us as a kind of dictation machine – that he inspires us, helps us and develops our gifting.

Bringing Up Boys

James Dobson

In his typically warm, compelling style, Dr James Dobson tackles the real questions that parents of boys are asking. Are boys really different from girls? How should boys be educated? What are the effects of divorce?

Providing insights on a wide variety of issues, Dr Dobson offers practical advice and encouragement for those shaping a new generation of men. He gives assurance that as they face a world filled with violence, lack of boundaries and conflicting rules of behaviour, boys can receive solid guidance from their parents and others who read and use this book.

Tyndale House
ISBN:0-8423-6929-5

Price:£7.99

£5.99 with voucher

First published in 2001 by Tyndale House
351 Executive Drive, Carol Stream, Wheaton, Illinois 60189, USA

Chapter 1

The Wonderful World Of Boys

Greetings to all the men and women out there who are blessed to be called parents. There is no greater privilege in living than bringing a tiny new human being into the world and then trying to raise him or her properly during the next eighteen years. Doing that job right requires all the intelligence, wisdom, and determination you will be able to muster from day to day. And for parents whose family includes one or more boys, the greatest challenge may be just keeping them alive through childhood and adolescence.

We have a delightful four-year-old youngster in our family named Jeffrey who is "all boy." One day last week, his parents and grandparents were talking in the family room when they realized that the child hadn't been seen in the past few minutes. They quickly searched from room to room, but he was nowhere to be found. Four adults scurried throughout the neighborhood calling, "Jeffrey? Jeffrey!" No answer. The kid had simply disappeared. Panic gripped the family as terrible possibilities loomed before them. Had he been kidnapped? Did he wander away? Was he in mortal danger? Everyone muttered a prayer while running from place to place. After about fifteen minutes of sheer terror, someone suggested they call 911. As they reentered the house, the boy jumped out and said, "Hey!" to his grandfather. Little Jeffrey, bless his heart, had been hiding under the bed while chaos swirled around him. It was his idea of a joke. He honestly thought everyone else would think it was funny too. He was shocked to learn that four big people were very angry at him.

Jeffrey is not a bad or rebellious kid. He is just a boy. And in case you haven't noticed, boys are different from girls. That fact was never in question for previous generations. They knew intuitively that each sex was a breed apart and that boys were typically the more unpredictable of the two. Haven't you heard your parents and grandparents say with a smile, "Girls are made out of sugar and spice and every-thing nice, but boys are made of snakes and snails and puppy-dog tails"? It was said tongue-in-cheek, but people of all ages thought it was based on fact. "Boys will be boys," they said knowingly. They were right.

Boys are usually (but not always) tougher to raise than their sisters are. Girls can be difficult to handle too, but there is something especially challenging about boys. Although individual temperaments vary, boys are designed to be more assertive, audacious, and excitable than girls are. Psychologist John Rosernond calls them "little aggressive machines."[1] One father referred to his son as all afterburner and no rudder. These are some of the reasons why Maurice Chevalier never sang, "Thank Heaven for Little Boys." They just don't inspire great sentimentality.

In an article entitled, "What Are Boys Made Of?" reporter Paula Gray Hunker quoted a mother named Meg

---

[1]   John Rosemond, as quoted in Paula Gray Hunker, 'What Are Boys Made Of?' *Washington Times*, 28 September 1999, 1(E).

MacKenzie who said raising her two sons is like living with a tornado. "From the moment that they come home from school, they'll be running around the house, climbing trees outside and making a commotion inside that sounds as if a herd of elephants has moved in upstairs. I'll try to calm them down, but my husband will say, 'This is what boys do. Get used to it.'"

Hunker continued, "Mrs. MacKenzie, the lone female in a household of males, says this tendency [of boys] to leap – and then listen – drives her crazy. 'I can't just tell my boys, "Clean up." If I do, they'll put one or two toys away and assume that the task is done. I've learned that I have to be very, very specific.' She has found that boys do not respond to subtle hints but need requests clearly outlined. 'I'll put a basket of clean laundry on the stairs, and the boys will pass it by twenty times and not once will it occur to them to stop and carry it upstairs,' she says."[2]

Does that sound familiar? If you host a birthday party for five-year-olds, the boys will probably behave very differently from the girls. One or more of them is likely to throw cake, put his hands in the punch bowl, or mess up the games for the girls. Why are they like this? Some would say their mischievous nature has been learned from the culture. Really? Then why are boys more aggressive in every society around the globe? And why did the Greek philosopher Plato write more than 2,300 years ago, "Of all the animals, the boy is the most unmanageable"?[3]

One of my favorite little books is entitled *Up to No Good: The Rascally Things Boys Do*, edited by Kitty Harmon. It is a compilation of stories told "by perfectly

[2] Ibid.
[3] Plato, *Laws*, 1953 edition 1, p. 164

decent grown men" recalling their childhood years. Here are several examples that made me smile:

> In seventh grade, the biology teacher had us dissect fetal pigs. My friends and I pocketed the snout of the pig and stuck it on the water fountain so that the water shot straight up out of the pig's nostrils. No one really noticed it until they were bent over just about to drink. The problem is that we wanted to stick around and see the results, but then we started laughing so hard that we got caught. We all got the paddle for that.
>
> Mark, Ohio, b. 1960

> A friend and I found a coffee can of gasoline in the garage and decided to pour some down a manhole, light it, and see what would happen. We popped the manhole open, poured some gas in, and replaced the cover so that it was ajar. We kept throwing matches down but nothing happened, so we poured all the gas in. Finally, there was a noise like a jet engine starting up, and then a big *BOOM!* The manhole cover flew up and a flame shot up about fifteen feet in the air. The ground was rumbling like an earthquake, and the manhole cover crashed about twelve feet away in the neighbor's driveway. What happened was the gas ran down the sewer lines for a block or so and vaporized with all the methane in there, and blew up all our neighbors' toilets. I'm a plumber now; that's how I know exactly what happened.
>
> Dave, Washington, b. 1952

> I am blind, and as a kid sometimes I played with other blind kids. And we always found just as many, or more, ways to get into trouble as sighted boys. Like the time I was over at a blind friend's house, and he took me into the garage to show me his older brother's motorcycle. We decided to take it out for a spin.

Why not? We rode down the street feeling for the curb, and at each intersection we'd stop, turn off the engine and listen, and then cross. We rode all the way to the high school track, where we could really let loose. First we piled up some dirt at the turns of the track so we'd feel the bump and know we were still on the track. Then we took off, going faster and faster and having a blast. What we didn't know was that people showed up to run on the track and were trying to wave us off. We couldn't hear them over the roar of the motorcycle engine and nearly ran them over. They called the police, who showed up and tried to wave us over too, but we kept going. Finally they got their sirens and bullhorns going and we stopped. They were furious and wouldn't believe us when we explained that we hadn't seen them. We proved we were blind by showing them our braille watches, and they escorted us home.

Mike, California, b. 1953[4]

As these stories illustrate, one of the scariest aspects of raising boys is their tendency to risk life and limb for no good reason. It begins very early. If a toddler can climb on it, he will jump off it. He careens out of control toward tables, tubs, pools, steps, trees, and streets. He will eat anything but food and loves to play in the toilet. He makes "guns" out of cucumbers or toothbrushes and likes digging around in drawers, pill bottles, and Mom's purse. And just hope he doesn't get his grubby little hands on a tube of lipstick. A boy harasses grumpy dogs and picks up kitties by their ears. His mom has to watch him

---

[4] Kitty Harmon, *Up to No Good: The Rascally Things Boys Do* (San Francisco Chronicle Books, 2000). From *Up to No Good: The Rascally Things Boys Do*, edited by Kitty Harmon. © 2000 by Tributary Books. Reprinted by permission of Chronicle Books, San Francisco.

every minute to keep him from killing himself. He loves to throw rocks, play with fire, and shatter glass. He also gets great pleasure out of irritating his brothers and sisters, his mother, his teachers, and other children. As he gets older, he is drawn to everything dangerous – skateboards, rock climbing, hang gliding, motorcycles, and mountain bikes. At about sixteen, he and his buddies begin driving around town like kamikaze pilots on sake. It's a wonder any of them survive. Not every boy is like this, of course, but the majority of them are.

Canadian psychologist Barbara Morrongiello studied the different ways boys and girls think about risky behavior. Females, she said, tend to think hard about whether or not they could get hurt, and they are less likely to plunge ahead if there is any potential for injury. Boys, however, will take a chance if they think the danger is worth the risk. Impressing their friends (and eventually girls) is usually considered worth the risk. Morrongiello shared a story about a mother whose son climbed on the garage roof to retrieve a ball. When she asked him if he realized he could fall, he said, "Well, I might not."[5]

A related study by Licette Peterson confirmed that girls are more fearful than boys are. For example, they brake sooner when riding their bikes. They react more negatively to pain and try not to make the same mistake twice. Boys, on the other hand, are slower to learn from calamities. They tend to think that their injuries were caused by "bad luck."[6] Maybe their luck will be better next time. Besides, scars are cool.

---

[5] Ira Dreyfus, 'Boys and Girls See Risk Differently, Study Says,' Associated Press, 16 February 1997
[6] Ibid.

Our son, Ryan, encountered one dangerous situation after another as a boy. By the time he was six, he was personally acquainted with many of the local emergency room attendants and doctors. And why not? He had been their patient repeatedly. One day when he was about four, he was running through the backyard with his eyes closed and fell into a decorative metal "plant." One of the steel rods stuck him in the right eyebrow and exposed the bone underneath. He came staggering through the back door bathed in blood, a memory that still gives Shirley nightmares. Off they went to the trauma center – again. It could have been much worse, of course. If the trajectory of Ryan's fall had been different by as much as a half inch, the rod would have hit him in the eye and gone straight to his brain. We have thanked God many times for the near misses.

I was also one of those kids who lived on the edge of disaster. When I was about ten, I was very impressed by the way Tarzan could swing through the trees from vine to vine. No one ever told me, "Don't try this at home." I climbed high into a pear tree one day and tied a rope to a small limb. Then I positioned myself for a journey to the next tree. Unfortunately, I made a small but highly significant miscalculation. The rope was longer than the distance from the limb to the ground. I kept thinking all the way down that something didn't seem right. I was still gripping the rope when I landed flat on my back twelve feet below and knocked all the air out of the state of Oklahoma. I couldn't breathe for what seemed like an hour (it must have been about ten seconds) and was sure I was dying. Two teeth were broken and a loud gonging sound echoed in my head. But later that afternoon, I was up and running again. No big deal.

The next year, I was given a chemistry set for Christmas. It contained no explosives or toxic materials, but in my hands, anything could be hazardous. I mixed some bright blue chemicals in a test tube and corked it tightly. Then I began heating the substance with a Bunsen burner. Very soon, the entire thing exploded. My parents had just finished painting the ceiling of my room a stark white. It was soon decorated with the most beautiful blue stuff, which remained splattered there for years. Such was life in the Dobson household.

It must be a genetic thing. I'm told my father was also a terror in his time. When he was a small boy, a friend dared him to crawl through a block-long drainpipe. He could only see a pinpoint of light at the other end, but he began inching his way into the darkness. Inevitably, I suppose, he became stuck somewhere in the middle. Claustrophobia swept over him as he struggled vainly to move. There he was, utterly alone and stranded in the pitch black pipe. Even if adults had known about his predicament, they couldn't have reached him. Rescue workers would have had to dig up the entire pipe to locate and get him out. The boy who was to become my dad finally made it to the other end of the drain and survived, thankfully, to live another day.

Two more illustrations: My father and all of his four brothers were high-risk kids. The two eldest were twins. When they were only three years old, my grandmother was shelling beans for the night meal. As my grandfather left for work, he said within hearing distance of the children, "Don't let the kids put those beans up their noses." Bad advice! As soon as their mom's back was turned, they stuffed their nasal passages with beans. It was impossible for my grandmother to get them out, so she just left them there. A few days later, the beans began to sprout. Little green shoots were actually growing out their nostrils. A family doctor worked diligently to dig out the tiny plants one piece at a time.

And years later, the five boys stood looking at an impressive steeple on a church. One of them dared the others to climb the outer side and see if they could touch the very highest point. All four of them headed up the structure like monkeys. My father told me that it was nothing but the grace of God that prevented them from tumbling from the heights. It was just a normal day in the life of five rambunctious little boys.

What makes young males act like that? What inner force compels them to teeter on the edge of disaster? What is it about the masculine temperament that drives boys to tempt the laws of gravity and ignore the gentle voice of common sense — the one that says, "Don't do it, Son"? Boys are like this because of the way they are wired neurologically and because of the influence of hormones that stimulate certain aggressive behavior. We will explore those complex and powerful masculine characteristics in the next chapter. You can't understand males of any age, including yourself or the one to whom you might be married, without knowing something about the forces that operate within.

We want to help parents raise "good" boys in this postmodern age. The culture is at war with the family, especially its youngest and most vulnerable members. Harmful and enticing messages are shouted at them from movies and television, from the rock-music industry, from the advocates of so-called safe-sex ideology, from homosexual activists, and from the readily available obscenity on the Internet. The question confronting parents is, "How can we steer our boys *and* girls past the many negative influences that confront them on every side?" It is an issue with eternal implications.

Our purpose in this regard will be to assist mothers and fathers as they "play defense" on behalf of their sons – that is, as they protect their boys from immoral and dangerous enticements. But that is not enough. Parents also need to "play offense" – to capitalize on the impressionable years of childhood by instilling in their sons the antecedents of character. Their assignment during two brief decades will be to transform their boys from immature and flighty youngsters into honest, caring men who will be respectful of women, loyal and faithful in marriage, keepers of commitments, strong and decisive leaders, good workers, and secure in their masculinity. And of course, the ultimate goal for people of faith is to give each child an understanding of Scripture and a lifelong passion for Jesus Christ. This is, I believe, *the* most important responsibility for those of us who have been entrusted with the care and nurturance of children.

Parents a century ago had a much better "fix" on these long-term objectives and how to achieve them. Some of their ideas are still workable today, and I will share them presently. I'll also provide a review of the latest research on child development and parent-child relationships. My prayer is that the findings and recommendations gleaned from that body of information, combined with my own professional experience spanning more than thirty years, will offer encouragement and practical advice to those who pass this way.

So buckle your seat belts. We have a lot of interesting ground to cover. But first, here's a little poem to get us started. It is taken from the lyrics to a song I love, sent to me by my friend Robert Wolgemuth. When Robert was a youngster, his mother, Grace Wolgemuth, sang "That Little Boy of Mine" to him and his siblings. I first heard it when Robert and his wife, Bobbie, sang it to my mother in 1983. A copyright search has turned up no information regarding the ownership of the lyrics and tune. To the best of their knowledge, Grace Wolgemuth's children believe that she created the song for them, and I am using it with their permission.

That Little Boy of Mine:

Two eyes that shine so bright
Two lips that kiss goodnite
Two arms that hold me tight
That little boy of mine.

No one could ever know, how much your coming has
*   meant*
To me you're everything. You 're something heaven
*   has sent*
You're all the world to me
You climb upon my knee
To me you'll always be
That little boy of mine.[7]

[7] 'That Little Boy of Mine,' used with permissi⟨ Wolgemuth.

Getting Anger Under Control

Neil Anderson

Our world has a serious problem with anger. Our offices and places of work have become hotbeds of hostility. Even retreating to the peace and safety of our homes doesn't appear to be an answer. Anger, impatience, frustration and incivility seem to have become standard behaviour in our society.

In the midst of this anger epidemic, here is a book which gets beyond mere anger management, to reveal true love, patience and kindness. It offers a way to resolve the personal and spiritual issues behind the anger and discover a peace of mind and heart running so deep and strong that it goes beyond human understanding.

Harvest House
ISBN: 0-7369-0349-6

Price:8.99

£6.99 with voucher

First published in 2002 by Harvest House
990 Owen Loop North, Eugene, Oregon
97402-9173, USA

Grace and Celebration

Can you put yourself in the prodigal's place for a moment? Can you see yourself squandering the good things God has given you, wasting your life in sin, desperately trying to survive? Then can you picture yourself coming to your senses and repenting, running to your Father? Filled with guilt for what you've done and shame for what you've become, can you hear yourself confessing your sin to Him?

But the father ... Once again, words of hope pour from the mouth of our gracious God! See the Father running to meet you, not wanting to miss one second of fellowship with you! See the compassion in His eyes! Feel the deep love in His warm, firm embrace, the joy in His kiss upon your cheek!

Can you feel your dignity and sense of worth being restored as He ignores your request to be made a servant? You are His son! There is no thought in the Father's heart that you would be anything but His son! Can you feel your heart burst with gratitude as He puts the robe and ring of honor on you and the sandals upon your tired, dusty feet? Welcome home!

Then the festive music and joyful dancing starts – the feast begins and the fattened calf is served. Smell the aroma! Taste the delicious food! See the eyes of your friends and your Father light up as you enter the room, and see the stunned look on your own face, because it's all for you! Child of God, it is a party in your honor!

Does this imagery surprise or even offend you? Is it hard for you to imagine having a party with God? Does it seem somehow "beneath" Him to revel and celebrate with such abandon? (Is it perhaps uncomfortably reminiscent of some of the ancient Greek myths about the riotous lives of their gods?)

The late Henri Nouwen, stunned by Rembrandt's painting *The Return of the Prodigal Son,* wrote about this side of God in his book by the same name.

> There is no doubt that the father [in the parable] wants a lavish feast. Killing the calf that had been fattened up for a special occasion shows how much the father wanted to pull out all the stops and offer his son a party such as had never been celebrated before. His exuberant joy is obvious. After having given his order to make everything ready, he exclaims: "We will celebrate by having a feast, because this son of mine was dead and has come back to life; he was lost and is found," and immediately they begin to celebrate ... I realize that I am not used to the image of God throwing a big party. It seems to contradict the solemnity and seriousness I have always attached to God. But when I think about the ways in which Jesus describes God's Kingdom, a joyful banquet is often at its center.[1]

Isn't that true? Jesus talked about people coming from the four corners of the earth to "recline at the table in the kingdom of God" (Luke 13:29). And told us that "the

---

[1] Henri Nouwen, *The Return of the Prodigal Son* (New York: Doubleday, 1994), pp. 112–113.

kingdom of heaven may be compared to a king who gave a wedding feast for his son" (Matthew 22:2). That theme is echoed in the book of Revelation when an angel declares to John, "Blessed are those who are invited to the marriage supper of the Lamb" (Revelation 19:9). In fact, the Bible says that God saved us and has us sitting right next to Him in heaven so that He can love on us and love on us some more, forever (Ephesians 2:4–7)!

This is God's free gift of love and kindness: From death to life. From lost to found. From disgrace to grace.

Dr. J.I. Packer, in his book *Knowing God*, wrote this about grace:

> The grace of God is love freely shown towards guilty sinners, contrary to their merit and indeed in defiance of their demerit. It is God showing goodness to persons who deserve only severity, and had no reason to expect anything but severity … It is surely clear that, once a man is convinced that his state and need are as described, the New Testament gospel of grace cannot but sweep him off his feet with wonder and joy. For it tells how our Judge has become our Savior.[2]

The Truth About Our God of Grace

The tragedy for so many believers in Christ, however, is that in their own perception their Savior has become their Judge. Having once known grace, they now experience guilt. Having once danced in the freedom of forgiveness, they now labor under a yoke of slavery to the law, seeking

---

[2] J. I. Packer, *Knowing God* (Downers Grove, IL: InterVarsity Press, 1973), p. 120.

desperately to please a seemingly unpleasable God. In their guilt they are angry – with God, at themselves, at the church, at preachers, at – you fill in the blanks. Who wouldn't be angry? After all, what is more frustrating than being expected to do the impossible?

Let's try to make some sense out of all this. First of all, assuming you are a child of God, what do you think Jesus' first words might be if He were to appear to you personally? "Shape up or ship out!" "Get your act together!" "Try harder!" "Why didn't you witness to that person today … or yesterday … or … ?"

While not wanting to put words in God's mouth, we believe that: Jesus would say something like this: "Grace and peace to you from God the Father." These words (or a similar greeting) begin 15 of the New Testament letters to churches and individuals. That greeting is not just the first-century version of "Hi, how are you?" It is a blessing from God, reminding the recipients of those God-breathed letters of their right standing before Him. They were standing in God's gracious presence arid were at peace with Him, and nothing could change that.

What an encouragement to know that, despite sins in their midst (yes, Paul greeted even the fleshly Corinthian church with "grace and peace to you" – twice!) and trials and perils in their lives (see Peter's letters), they were forgiven, accepted, and affirmed. Completely. Irrevocably. Eternally.

Why is there so often an intense battle in our minds to believe that truth? We believe it is because the enemy of our souls knows that we will be unable to grow spiritually or bear fruit if we do not truly believe we are forgiven children of God. Listen to Peter's words about God's work:

By [His own glory and excellence, God] has granted to us His precious and magnificent promises, so that by them you may become partakers of the divine nature, having escaped the corruption that is in the world by lust. Now for this very reason also, applying all diligence, in your faith supply moral excellence, and in your moral excellence, knowledge, and in your knowledge, self control, and in your self-control, perseverance, and in your perseverance, godliness, and in your godliness, brotherly kindness, and in your brotherly kindness, love. For if these qualities are yours and are increasing, they render you neither useless nor unfruitful in the true knowledge of our Lord Jesus Christ. *For he who lacks these qualities is blind or short-sighted, having forgotten his purification from his former sins*

(2 Peter 1:4–9, emphasis added).

Did you catch the impact of Peter's message? He declared that it is a real and present danger to lose sight of the forgiveness we have in Christ! And if we do, then we will not develop spiritual disciplines, we will not grow, and we will not bear fruit.

Remembering His Grace

Perhaps the condition that Peter describes is the one you find yourself in today. If so, God wants you to be reminded of your purification from your former sins. He wants you to know His grace and peace once again. He wants you to know that you are indeed forgiven and are a new creation in Christ. Consider the following Scriptures:

Who is a God like you, who pardons sin and forgives the transgression of the remnant of his inheritance? You do not stay angry forever but delight to show mercy. You will again have compassion on us; you will tread our sins underfoot and hurl all our iniquities into the depths of the sea

(Micah 7:18–19 NIV).

The Lord is compassionate and gracious, slow to anger, abounding in love. He will not always accuse, nor will he harbor his anger forever; he does not treat us as our sins deserve or repay us according to our iniquities. For as high as the heavens are above the earth, so great is his love for those who fear him; as far as the east is from the west, so far has he removed our transgressions from us

(Psalm 103:8–12 NIV).

He was pierced through for our transgressions, He was crushed for our iniquities; the chastening for our well-being fell upon Him, and by His scourging we are healed. All of us like sheep have gone astray, each of us has turned to his own way; but the LORD has caused the iniquity of us all to fall on Him

(Isaiah 53:5–6).

"This is the covenant that I will make with them after those days, says the LORD: I will put My laws upon their heart, and on their mind I will write them," He then says, "And their sins and their lawless deeds I will remember no more." Now where there is forgiveness of these things, there is no longer any offering for sin

(Hebrews 10:16–18).

When you were dead in your transgressions and the uncircumcision of your flesh, He made you alive together with Him, having forgiven us all our transgressions, having canceled out the certificate of debt consisting of decrees against us, which was hostile to us; and He has taken it out of the way, having nailed it to the cross

(Colossians 2:13–15).

"Come now, and let us reason together," says the LORD, "though your sins are as scarlet, they will be as white as snow; though they are red like crimson, they will be like wool"

(Isaiah 1:18).

"I have wiped out your transgressions like a thick cloud, and your sins like a heavy mist. Return to Me, for I have redeemed you"

(Isaiah 44:22).

The imagery that God has given us in the Scriptures of His forgiveness could not be more vivid. He forgives and re-members our sins no more. He laid every last one of them on Christ and nailed them to the cross with Him. God has holy amnesia when it comes to all our wrongdoing. He has driven our sins away like the breeze blowing away the morning fog.

Child of God, you are forgiven! You are free! You are alive in Christ!

"Paid in Full"

Do yourself a favor. Take out a piece of paper and write down every wrong thing whose guilt still haunts you. The things you should have done but didn't. The things you shouldn't have done but did. Write down every bit of anger that you still harbor against God, yourself, and others.

Then write the words "PAID IN FULL" in red letters across that paper. That is the literal translation of the heart cry of Jesus on the cross when He said, "*Tetelestai!*" Often rendered "It is finished!" (see John 19:30), it is our Lord's exclamation point to His sacrificial death that paid the complete penalty of death for our sins.

It is over.

Now take that paper and do something with it that will stay in your memory. Trample on it. Rip it to shreds. Burn it. Tie it around a rock, go out in your boat, and throw it into the deepest part of a lake. Whatever you do, know that you are only acting out symbolically what God in Christ has already done for you, by grace, forever.

Please join us in this prayer:

Dear heavenly Father, grace and truth came through Your Son, Jesus Christ. And I have received of His fullness, grace upon grace. I don't want to be like the nine ungrateful lepers who were healed but never came back to express their gratitude to Jesus. So I say "Thank You, Lord!" for the grace and mercy You lavished upon me in Christ. Make today a landmark day for me so that I will never forget the forgiveness that is mine in Him. Give me discernment to recognize the accuser's lies, by which he seeks to drag me again into the gutter of guilt. I renounce all his deception and choose to believe the truth of what You have done for me. Heal my damaged emotions, Lord. In Jesus' name I pray, amen.

Nothing Like a Dame

Thora Hird

From her birth in 1911 to the present day, Dame Thora Hird tells her life story in this humorous autobiography, covering her varied career, her family and her strong faith in God.

Thora's story brings us affectionate reminiscences, from the early days of being 'spotted' by George Formby to her BAFTA-winning performances for Alan Bennett's Talking Heads. Theatrical anecdotes guide us through her West End successes and film roles and she recalls with fondness her well-loved television series, including Praise Be! and Last of the Summer Wine.

Widely acknowledged for her work, she also talks about her wonderful marriage to husband, Scottie, the achievements of her daughter, Janette, and the support of her friends who surround her.

Zondervan
ISBN:0-00-710766-8

Price:£6.99

£4.99 with voucher

First published in 2001 by Zondervan Publishing
5300 Paterson Avenue Street, Grand Rapids,
Michigan 49530, USA

5.

We never closed

'Are you there, Mrs Hird?'

This enquiry always followed a quick knock on our front door, which was always open, that is from about eight o'clock in a morning until eleven or later at night, when my mother would say, very dramatically, 'Have you locked the front door, Jim?'

I must admit there was no need to lock the front door because we really had nothing of great value to pinch! Well, no, that's not quite fair of me really. There were things like the piano, my dad's various banjos, our Nev's many musical instruments, my mother's very tiny diamond earrings and silver coffee set, which an aunt had left to her when she had passed away.

Apart from those, everything else was only of great sentimental value, although, really, those *are* the most valuable of all one's possessions I think! But, 'Have you locked the front door, Jim?' was always said with such dramatic feeling that after my mother had been assured, we were able to go to our beds and sleep peacefully and safely (even though the back kitchen door was never locked because it couldn't be as there was never a lock on it!)

So, our front door was open, eight to eleven. I'd like to think the Windmill Theatre derived its slogan 'We Never Closed' from us. But it didn't.

Rat-tat!

'Are you there, Mrs Hird?' If I had a shilling for every time I had heard that, or, 'Can I come in for a minute, Mrs Hird?' or 'Are you in, Mrs Hird?', I'd be well off.

'There's no doubt my mother was a Living Wonder – her great big heart seemed to beat solely for the purpose of helping people, and I sometimes try to comfort myself by thinking it was not surprising that she died when she was only sixty-two, of heart trouble, because she had used her loving heart so very much – it was tired out.

When she did die, there was a hush of respect and loss in the whole district and it is with the same feeling and great pride' that I pen this next bit. 'Are you there, Mrs Hird?' As I say, there would be a quick 'Rat-tat' on the front door, the enquiry as to whether my mother was in (which in itself was a laugh as she hardly ever went out!) and then there would be one of the following various requests, 'Can you lend my mother an eggcupful of tea please?' or 'Please, Mrs Hird, can you lend me two candles?' or, offering the teacup they held in their hand 'Can you lend me a drop of vinegar?' or, a frequent request, 'Mrs Hird, me mother says have you please got a piece of brown paper and some string, she wants to send a parcel?'

My memories of these daily requests are very warm and loving ones and I can still remember my mother's soft smile as she would say, 'Yes, of course, love,' to the tea, candles or vinegar type of requests and 'Just a minute, love, I'll have a look,' to the brown paper and string appeal. (I still carefully fold a piece of good brown paper and I have a biscuit tin painted red that houses good pieces of string – not that it's likely anyone is going to knock on our door and request either, but I suppose old habits die hard, and even in this Sellotape age it's amazing how often one uses brown paper and string – and it would be great if one of my splendid neighbours were ever in need and I could oblige. I don't think they ever *will* be – because I'll bet they save nice big pieces of brown paper and good lengths of string. Who doesn't?)

I recall one afternoon when there was the usual rat-tat on the door and a voice called, 'Oh, can you come a minute, Mrs Hird, the baby's had a fit!'

Off went my mother. She wasn't a nurse or anything – the frightened mother of the baby knew this – but the fact that my mother was *there* until the Doctor arrived was all the young mother wanted.

Another type of 'non-paying customer' – and there were dozens of these, bless 'em – would knock on the door without calling out to see if my mother was 'There' or 'In' or anything else. This type would remain at the open front door until my mother answered the knock by joining them. 'Oh hello, So and So,' my mother would say and then after an answering, 'Hello, Mrs Hird' the dialogue would usually run something like this:

'Er – sorry to trouble you, Mrs Hird, but I'm going to a Fancy Dress Ball as a gypsy on Friday' at the Ambulance Hall (or "The Albert Hall" – oh, yes, we had an Albert Hall in Morecambe – or "The Tower" we'd one of those 'as well!) and will you make my face up please?'

There was never any hesitation on my mother's part. 'Of course I will, love, what time does it start?'

'Eight o'clock,' the would-be gypsy would reply.

'All right, you'd better come here about seven and – oh – have you got plenty of beads and some brass curtain rings for earrings?' 'Well, no,' would be the doleful reply. 'Oh well, don't worry. I'll get out the bead box and you can choose which you would like after I've made you up, love!'

I must add at this point that the 'Fancy Dress Ballers' who called weren't always going to the Ball as gypsies. Oh no, we were perruquiers and make-up artists to Grecians, Italians, Romans, Red Indians, clowns and ... all for love! Never mind about 'We Never Closed!' We Never *Charged* either!

That was my mother's principle and, as she would say to my dad, 'Well, Jim, if it's giving them a bit of pleasure!' To which James Henry would reply, 'You'll kill yourself doing for other people. You never stop, you're so soft, you'll run when the dog won't!'

I never knew the meaning of that remark but one thing I *did* know, he wouldn't have had my mother any different!

The prizewinning request for help came one Sunday. There was the usual rat-tat and, 'Are you there, Mrs Hird?' followed by a tearful young neighbour coming along the passage into our living-kitchen.

'Now then,' said my mother, her own face looking as sad and troubled as the young neighbour's, 'what ever's the matter, love?'

The young woman wiped her eyes and blew her running nose and amidst sobs informed us that her young husband's father and mother had turned up unexpectedly. (I can vouch for the unexpected bit – if you live at the seaside you are expected to run a free boarding house for relatives and always have enough food in to feed 'em!) However, her in-laws had turned up for the day and she and her husband had had their dinner, two chops, half an hour ago, and as it was the in-laws' first visit since she'd married their loving son, she wanted to impress them.

Stopping to have another nose blow and wipe the tears away she said, 'I – er – feel awful asking you this, Mrs Hird – but have you done a roast?'

Isn't the Lancashire idiom lovely? 'Have you *done* a roast?' *not* 'Have you roasted a joint?' My mother looked at the young wife. 'Yes,' she said, 'as a matter of fact I was just going to carve – why?' 'Well – er,' and the tears flowed again. 'Could you lend it to me – I do want to create a good impression – I'll bring it back after!'

My mother's eyes did a quick side glance at my father – he was sitting by the fire reading the Sunday paper. He was no help – he didn't even look up, he knew what the result would be, and he wasn't reading either – I could see that – he was thinking!

'Now don't upset yourself like that,' my mother comforted as she darted into the back kitchen. She immediately produced a large black japanned tray from down by 'the side of the old fashioned kitchen dresser. Placing the tray on the top of the dresser, the part of the dresser she baked or cut bread on etc., the next move was to the gas stove against the opposite wall. Quick as a flash, the still-sizzling joint of sirloin beef on its meat plate was transferred to the tray.

Plonk! I can still hear that meat plate landing on the tray as I write this – and I can still remember my dad's expression as he very carefully and deliberately folded the *Sunday Chronicle* and put it down.

'You'd better take the vegetables as well,' my mother was saying, as vegetable dishes of steaming goodness' were lifted off the plate rack on the stove where they had been keeping warm. The next item was the gravy – which my mother always made in the meat roasting tin, using all the lovely succulent juices of the roasted meat as a base. By this time my dear father was in a state of trance or at least that's what he looked like. Next item on the menu? A large apple pie and a glass jug of custard waltzed their way onto the tray, as my mother was advising, 'And you'd better go out the back way, love, then nobody will see you!'

During that bit of the drama the dresser drawer was opened and a spotless white towel whisked out and laid Over the large trayful of food. Amid sniffs of gratitude and thanks, 'the lucky winner was saying, 'Ooo, you are good, Mrs Hird. I don't know what we'd all do without you – ooo, you are that kind,' etc., etc. And out she went, the back way.

Now you know the sort of silence that hits you? We experience it at our little country place at night – one can almost 'hear the silence'. Right, that was the atmosphere in our house after the sizzling sirloin, roasted potatoes, cauliflower, peas, roasted parsnips, carrots and light-as-fluff Yorkshire puds, not to mention the apple pie and custard, had made their exit, the back way! Neville and I had never uttered a sound during the entire pantomime – we knew better. We also knew this was typical of our mother, and we also knew from experience the expression on Dad's face!

There was a deathly hush. In fact Nev and I were nearly at our tittering stage, because James Henry Hird was standing 'looking at nothing', chin in air; he looked as though he was contemplating the narrow border of wallpaper that divided the paper on the wall from the two foot frieze. He was what is known as 'containing himself'. After what seemed about two days, but was actually about half a minute, my mother, who was still in the back kitchen, started to sing a few bars of 'Oh, where is my boy tonight?' – very softly, of course, and then, just as though nothing unusual had happened or as though it was the normal routine to go to all that trouble to cook a big dinner for your loved ones and then give it away before they'd even sampled it, she called out, 'Can you eat *two* fried eggs with your bacon, Jim, love?'

By now, my father was viewing the table, almost as though he'd never seen it before – the white linen doth, places set for four people, Victorian silver cruet (cleaned by yours truly every Friday!), linen serviettes in our individual rings.

'Can you eat two fried eggs with your bacon, Jim, love?'
'Yes, please,' replied James Henry in the voice he used when playing kings or Roman emperors – while still contemplating the table. 'They'll be very nice with horseradish sauce!'

Lies Women Believe and The Truth That Sets Them Free

Nancy Leigh DeMoss

Author Nancy Leigh DeMoss believes that the lies Christian women believe are at the heart of most of their struggles.

"Many women live under a cloud of personal guilt and condemnation," says DeMoss. "Many are in bondage to their past. Others are gripped by a fear of rejection and a longing for approval. Still others are emotional prisoners."

In this book, DeMoss exposes the areas of deception most commonly believed by Christian women – lies about God, sin, priorities, marriage and family, emotions and more. She then sheds light on how they can be delivered from bondage and set free to walk in God's grace, forgiveness and abundant life.

Moody Press
ISBN: 0-8024-7296-6

Price: £9.99

£7.99 With voucher

Published by Moody Press
820 North Lasalle Boulevard, Chicago, Illinois
60610-3284, USA

38

'MY CIRCUMSTANCES WILL NEVER CHANGE – THIS WILL GO ON FOREVER.'

This lie imprisons many women in hopelessness and despair.

The Truth is, your pain – be it physical affliction, memories of abuse, a troubled marriage, or a heart broken by a wayward child – may go on for a long time. But it will not last forever. It may go on for all of your life down here on this earth. But even a lifetime is not forever.

The Truth is, a moment or two from now (in the light of eternity), when we are in the presence of the Lord, everything that has taken place in this life will be just a breath – a comma.

A woman called a few days ago and asked for counsel in dealing with a complicated and painful situation in her marriage. The situation had been that way for as long as she could remember, and there was no indication of anything changing in the future. In the course of the conversation, I was moved as this dear, suffering wife said, "If it goes on for our whole lives, that's OK. I know that time is short and eternity is long. One day this will all be just a blip on the screen." She spoke not as one who is just resigned to her "fate." She longs for things to be different now. But she has a perspective of time and eternity that is enabling her to be faithful in the midst of the "fire."

Another woman came to me years ago after a conference and said, "I want to thank you for what you said about being faithful to your mate, no matter what." She went on to tell the story of how she had lived for forty years in a marriage to a wicked man. She said, "All through those years, many people – including well-meaning Christians – counseled me to get out of this marriage. But somehow, God kept drawing me back to that vow I had made, and I did not believe it was right to leave." After a pause, she continued, "I'm so glad I waited. You see, a year ago, my husband finally got saved, and God is truly changing him, after all these years. And not only that," she said softly, with tears in her eyes, "you can't believe the incredible changes God has brought about in *my* life as a result of the suffering."

The problem is, we are so earthbound that, to most of us, forty years sounds like *eternity!* We can't fathom enduring that long. If we could only see that forty years – or longer – is inconsequential in the light of eternity.

Regardless of how long our suffering continues, God's Word assures us that it will not last forever.

> Therefore we do not Jose heart ... For our light and *momentary troubles* are achieving for us an eternal glory that far outweighs them all. So we our eyes not on what is seen, but on what is unseen. For *what is seen* [i.e., our current trouble] *is temporary*, but what is unseen [i.e., the glory that awaits us] is eternal.
> *2 Corinthians 4:16–18, italics added*

> I consider that our present sufferings are not worth comparing
> with the glory that will be revealed in us.
>
> *Romans 8:18*

> Weeping may endure for a night, but joy cometh in the
> morning.
>
> *Psalm 30:5* kjv

Your night of weeping may go on for months or even
years. But if you are a child of God, it will not go on forever.
God has determined the exact duration of your suffering,
and it will not last one moment longer than He knows is
necessary to achieve His holy, eternal purposes in and
through your life.

In those cases where there is no relief from pain in this
life, we have literally hundreds of promises in God's Word
that one day all suffering will be over, faith will become
sight, darkness will be turned to light, and our faithfulness
will be rewarded with unending joy. He promises that one
day,

> [the] desert and the parched land will be glad;
> the wilderness will rejoice and blossom ...
> And the ransomed of the Lord ...
> will enter Zion with singing;
> everlasting joy will crown their heads.
> Gladness and joy will overtake them,
> and sorrow and sighing will flee away.
>
> *Isaiah 35:1, 10*

Regardless of how powerful the forces of darkness seem to
be here and now, the final chapter has been written – and
God wins! Believing the Truth about what lies ahead will

fill us with hope and enable us to persevere between now and then.

39

'I JUST CAN'T TAKE ANY MORE.'

Here is another lie the Enemy works hard to get us to believe, because he knows if we do, we will live in defeat and hopelessness. One woman wrote and said:

> *I have one-year-old twin boys who have been chronically sick with ear infections and colds for two months, causing them to he whiny and irritable constantly. I kept telling myself my husband, and anyone who would listen, "I can't take it anymore." The lie was a self-fulfilling prophecy, and it was stressing me out. When I finally said, "Yes, I can take it and I will do my duty to them," the greatest part of the tension and stress I was feeling dissolved.*

All of us have had seasons when we feel we just can't keep going; we just can't take any more. As with every other area of deception, the key to defeating this lie is to counter it with the Truth. Regardless of what our emotions or our circumstances may tell us, God's Word says, "My grace is sufficient for you" (2 Corinthians 12:9).

Most of us are familiar with that verse. But, when it comes to the circumstances and trials of our lives, few of us really believe it. What we really believe is, "I can't go on ...

- I can't take one more sleepless night with this sick child;
- I can't continue in this marriage;
- I can't bear to be hurt one more time by my mother-in-law;
- I can't keep making it with three teenagers and a mother with Alzheimer's living in our home ..."

However, whether I choose to believe it or not, if I am His child, the Truth is that "His grace *is* sufficient for me." (This is assuming, of course, that I haven't taken on myself responsibilities He never intended me to carry. If the burden is God-given, I can go on by His grace.) His grace is sufficient for every moment, every circumstance, every detail, every need, and every failure of my life.

When I'm exhausted and think I can't possibly face the unfinished tasks that are still before me, *His grace is sufficient for me.*

When I'm having a hard time responding to that family member or that person at the office who really gets under my skin, *His grace is sufficient for me.*

When I am tempted to vent my frustration by speaking harsh words, *His grace is sufficient for me.*

When I've given in to my lust for food for the umpteenth time that day, *His grace is sufficient for me.*

When I blow it with my family and become uptight and even peevish, *His grace is sufficient for me.*

When I don't know which direction to go or what decision to make, *His grace is sufficient for me.*

When my heart is breaking with an overwhelming sense of loss and grief as I stand by the grave of a loved one, *His grace is sufficient for me.*

What do you need God's grace for? Wayward children? Aching body? Unloving husband? No money in the bank? Struggling to raise three kids without a dad in the home? Don't know where next month's rent is coming from? Lost your job? Just moved to a new city and don't know a soul? Church going through a split? Desperately lonely? Weighed down with guilt? Chemically dependent? Hormones going haywire?

Fill in the blank. Whatever your story, whatever your situation, right now, *His grace is sufficient for you.* His divine resources are available to meet your need — no matter how great. That's the Truth. And the Truth will set you free.

Dear child of God, your heavenly Father will never lead you anywhere that His grace will not sustain you. He will never place more upon you than He will give you grace to bear. When the path before you seems hopelessly long, take heart. Lift up your eyes. Look ahead to that day when all suffering will be over. And remember that when you stand before Him, all the tears and sorrows of a lifetime will seem dim in comparison with the beauty and glory of His face. Without a doubt, you will say, "His amazing grace has brought me safely home."

40

'IT'S ALL ABOUT ME.'

Lying on my desk are two advertisements – one for a national stationery supplier, the other for a large chain of retail stores. The head line for both ads reads:

It's all about you.

The philosophy behind those ad campaigns is almost as old as the human race. In effect, that's exactly what the Serpent said to Eve: "It's all about *you*." It's a campaign he has been running effectively ever since.

One writer observed that "to most people the greatest persons in the universe are themselves. Their lives are made up of endless variations on the word 'me."[fn8]

It's true. In spite of all the talk about poor self-image, our instinctive reaction to life is self-centered: How does this affect *me?* Will this make *me* happy? Why did this have to happen to *me?* What does she think about *me?* It's *my* turn. Where's *my* share? Nobody cares about *my* ideas. He hurt *my* feelings. I've got to have some time for *me*. I need *my* space. He's not sensitive to *my* needs.

It's not enough for us to be the center of our own universe. We want to be the center of everyone else's universe as well – including God's. When others don't bow down before us and devote themselves to promoting our happiness and meeting our needs, we get hurt and start looking for alternate ways to fulfill our egocentric agenda.

You'd think the church would be the one place where
things would revolve around God rather than man. But not
necessarily so. In his book *Finding God*, Dr. Larry Crabb
offers a penetrating analysis of the extent to which the
evangelical church has given in to this deception:

Helping people to feel loved and worthwhile has become the
central mission of the church. We are learning not to worship
God in self-denial and costly service, but to embrace our inner
child, heal our memories, overcome addictions, lift our
depressions, improve our self-images, establish self-preserving
boundaries, substitute self-love for self – hatred, and replace
shame with an affirming acceptance of who we are.

Recovery from pain is absorbing an increasing share of the
church's energy. And that is alarming ...

We have become committed to relieving the pain behind
our problems rather than using our pain to wrestle more
passionately with the character and purpose of God. *Feeling
better has become more important than finding God ...*

As a result, we happily camp on biblical ideas that help us
feel loved and accepted, and we pass over Scripture that calls us
to higher ground. We twist wonderful truths about God's
acceptance, his redeeming love, and our new identity in Christ
into a basis for honoring ourselves rather than seeing those
truths for what they are: the stunning revelation of a God
gracious enough to love people who hated him, a God worthy
to be honored above everyone and everything else.

... We have rearranged things so that God is now worthy of
honor because he has honored us. "Worthy is the Lamb," we
cry, not in response to his amazing grace, but because he has
recovered what we value most: the ability to like ourselves.
We now matter more than God.[1]

The apostle Paul understood that God does not exist for us, but that we exist for Him:

> By him all things were created: things in heaven and on earth, visible and invisible, whether thrones or powers or rulers or authorities; all things were created by him and for him. He is before all things, and in all things hold together. And he is the head of the body, the church; he is the beginning and the first-born from among the dead, so that in everything he might have the supremacy.
>
> *Colossians 1:16–18*

Why was Paul able to sing hymns to God in the middle of the night from the belly of a Roman dungeon? How could he stay faithful and "rejoice always," while being stoned, shipwrecked, lied about, and rejected by friends and enemies alike? How could he "rejoice always" when he was hungry and tired? His secret was that he had settled the issue of why he was living. He was not living to please himself or to get his needs fulfilled. From the point of his conversion on the road to Damascus, he had one burning passion: to live for the glory and the pleasure of God. All that mattered to him was knowing Christ and making Him. known to others.

> I consider my life worth nothing to me, if only
> I may finish the race and complete the task
> the Lord Jesus has given me – the task of
> testifying to the gospel of God's grace.
>
> *Acts 20:24*

The bottom line for Paul was: "To live is Christ." Once that was settled, nothing else mattered much.

CORAM DEO

Coram Deo is a Latin phrase that means "before the face of God." Many years ago, a woman sent me a framed piece on which she had written out in calligraphy a succinct reminder of what it means to function as our Creator designed us to live:

> CORAM DEO
> Living all of life
> in the presence of God
> under the authority of God
> and to the glory of God.

I want to close this chapter by sharing with you three sketches of women who exemplify what it means to live *coram Deo*.

"Cindy" shared her story with me in a lengthy letter. She got married at the age of eighteen and had three children by the time she was twenty-one. Though she had been baptized as a child, she did not know what it was to have a personal relationship with Jesus Christ. When she was in her thirties, as her mother lay in a hospital in a coma, dying of cancer, Cindy picked up a Gideon Bible and cried out to the Lord to help her. "From that moment on," she wrote, "my heart's desire was to know God."

Over the next several years, her marriage and family life became increasingly rocky. There was a vicious cycle of abusive behavior and language; her fourteen-year-old daughter ran away from home and her two sons were in consistent trouble at school and with the police. At one point, Cindy left her husband for two weeks, intending to divorce him; through a series of circumstances, God gave her a new compassion for him, and she returned home.

In the midst of all the turmoil at home, Cindy attended a meeting at a nearby church, where she heard the Good News of God's love and how Jesus died to save sinners. She gave her heart to Jesus and became a new creature.

Things continued to get worse at home. Her children, now in their teens, were completely out of control. Her daughter ended up on the streets for a year, after her dad would not let her back in the house one day. Subsequently, the daughter married and had five children; she is now going through a divorce, after twenty-five years of marriage. Her father has never been willing to talk to her and does not know his grandchildren or great-grandchildren.

One son was dishonorably discharged from the Marines and spent four years in prison; he and his father are estranged and have not spoken in years.

The other son became a drug addict and was also dishonorably discharged from the military. He was involved in a homicide in a tavern and spent twenty-two years in a penitentiary. Though he made a profession of faith while in prison, he no longer shows any interest in spiritual things.

Cindy concluded her letter by reflecting on the needs in her family and where she fits in to all that is going on:

There are no Christmases or Thanksgivings here at home. Will my family ever be healed emotionally and spiritually? Only the Lord knows. But God is Lord of my life, and I believe He wants to use me to be a testimony and a light for my family. If I don't show them the truth of God's amazing grace, who will? It would be so easy to just walk away and go to some island where there is peace and joy. But God has chosen me to be where I am, to be a testimony to my unsaved husband and to my children.

How can I help my husband see that one day his pride will be taken away and he will have to face Christ? How can I help my daughter see the truth of God's unconditional love? How can I help my eldest son, who has turned his back on God since leaving prison? How can I help my husband reconcile with his other son and daughter? Only through God's power, wisdom, and love. So with all my heart, mind, body, and soul, I say, "Yes, Lord – whatever You want me to do."

Jennie Thompson is a young woman whose husband went to be with the Lord not long ago, after an intense two-year battle with leukemia. In a letter written three months after Robert's home-going, this widow with four boys ages seven and under expresses an extraordinary perspective on the heart and purposes of God:

The Lord has been faithful in holding us up through this time. I wouldn't in a million years have chosen this path for my life or the lives of my children, but we have learned so much in and though our circumstances that we could never have learned another way. God has been honored and glorified in a way that never could have happened without our circumstances, so I must praise Him for those circumstances.

God is not in the business of making us "happy"; His business is to receive the glory that is due Him as our Creator and almighty God. Our happiness is the by-product of being in and doing His will. That, and only that, is the reason I can be weeping at the graveside of my best friend, my husband, and the father of my children and still be happy.

In the fall of 1998, my dear friend and longtime prayer partner **Janiece Grissom** began to experience numbness and tingling in her hands and then her arms. Early in 1999, after many tests and doctor appointments, a neurologist confirmed that she had Lou Gehrig's disease. Janiece was forty-one years old and the mother of four children, ages four to twelve.

Over the next ten months, the disease took over first one part and then another of her steadily weakening body. Throughout those months, as we had occasion to talk on the phone, Janiece always refused to focus on herself or her prognosis. Invariably, when she would hear my voice, she would say, "Nancy, you've really been on my heart! How can I pray for you?"

In October of that year, I visited with Janiece and her husband in their home in Little Rock. By this time, she was confined to a recliner; she could not use her arms or legs and could speak only with difficulty, as she had lost 50 percent of her lung capacity. Again, I was deeply touched by how God-conscious and God-centered this couple was, even as they faced the ravages of this disease. I remember Janiece saying over and over that evening, "God has been so good to us!" As the evening drew to a close, several of us surrounded her chair, prayed together, and then sang one of her favorite hymns:

> Like a river glorious is God's perfect peace …
> Stayed upon Jehovah, hearts are fully blest –
> Finding as He promised, perfect peace and rest.[2]

Within the next week, Janiece's physical condition began to deteriorate even more rapidly. Because she was unable to swallow, she was taken to the hospital to have a feeding tube inserted. She never returned home. On the evening of December 13, I called her husband to see how she was doing. Her strength was almost gone, and she could not speak above a whisper. "But," Tim said, "the incredible thing is that she is still spending most of her waking hours praying for other people." Within a matter of hours, Janiece breathed her last and was in the presence of the Lord.

Janiece Grissom died the way she had lived – selflessly loving God and others. In her mind, it was never about herself – her health, her comfort, her future. It was all about God – all that mattered was glorifying Him through surrendering to His purposes for her life. Her sole desire, as expressed by the apostle Paul, was that "now as always Christ will be exalted in my body, whether by life or by death" (Philippians 1:20).

Pastor's wife and author Susan Hunt says it beautifully:

> History is the story of redemption. This story is much bigger than I. I am not the main character in the drama of redemption. I am not the point. But by God's grace I am a part of it. My subplot is integral to the whole. It is far more significant to have a small part in this story than to star in my own puny production. This is a cosmic story that will run throughout eternity. Will I play my part with grace and joy, or will I go for the short-run, insignificant story that really has no point?[3]

The Truth is, it's not about you. It's not about me. It's all about Him. The Truth may not change your circumstances – at least not here and now – but it will change *you*. The Truth will set you free.

Notes

[1] Larry Crabb, *Finding God* (Grand Rapids: Zondervan, 1993), 17–18

[2] Francis R. Havergal, 'Like a River Glorious.'

[3] Susan Hunt, The True Woman (Wheaton, Ill.: Crossway, 1997), 75.

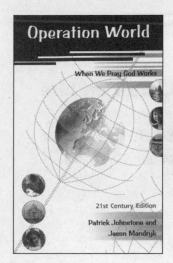

Operation World
Patrick Johnstone

£9.99 with voucher

~~£14.99~~
1 8507.8357 8

Lucas on Life

Jeff Lucas

£4.99 **with voucher**

~~£6.99~~

1 8602.4360 6

Live Like a Jesus Freak
dc Talk

£5.99 with voucher

~~£7.99~~
0 8634.7501 9

Shannon
Shannon Ribeiro & Damaris Kofmehl

£4.99 with voucher

~~£6.99~~
0 3407.8648 5

Unquenchable Worshipper

Matt Redman

£3.99 with voucher

~~£4.99~~

0 8547.6995 1

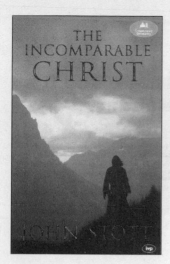

Incomparable Christ

John Stott

£6.99 **with voucher**

~~£8.99~~

0 8511.1485 7

Mark for Everyone

Tom Wright

£6.99 **with voucher**

~~£8.99~~

0 2810.5299 9

Thank God It's Monday

Mark Greene

£3.99 with voucher

~~£5.99~~
1 8599.9503 9

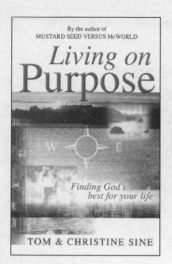

Living on Purpose

Tom and Christine Sine

£5.99 with voucher

~~£7.99~~

1 8542.4520 1

Travels with a Primate

Terry Waite

£5.99 with voucher

~~£7.99~~

0-0071.0633-5

Christ Empowered Living

Selwyn Hughes

£3.99 with voucher

~~£5.99~~

1 8534.5201 7

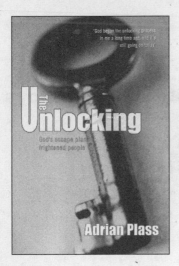

Unlocking

Adrian Plass

£4.99 with voucher

£6.99

0 7459.3510 9

Behind the Songs

(with FREE CD)

Graham Kendrick

£7.99 with voucher

£12.99

1 8400.3735 0

Bringing Up Boys

James Dobson

£5.99 **with voucher**

~~£7.99~~

0 8423.6929 5

Getting Anger Under Control

Neil Anderson

£6.99 with voucher

£8.99

0 7369.0349 6

Nothing Like a Dame

Thora Hird

£4.99 with voucher

£6.99

0 0071.0766 8

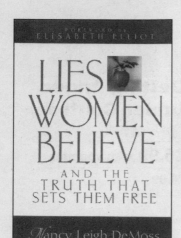

Lies Women Believe

Nancy Leigh DeMoss

£7.99 with voucher

~~£9.99~~

0-8024.7296-6

Get Caught Reading...

the Word

vouchers

---

1 8507.8357 8

£5 off *Operation World*

This 'Get Caught Reading...the **Word**' voucher £5 is redeemable against the purchase of *Operation World (Authentic Lifestyle)* in all bookshops participating in the promotion. Offer valid until 30th June 2002. Voucher cannot be exchanged for cash or any other merchandise.

---

1 8602.4360 6

£2 off *Lucas On Life*

This 'Get Caught Reading...the **Word**' voucher £2 is redeemable against the purchase of *Lucas On Life (Authentic Lifestyle)* in all bookshops participating in the promotion. Offer valid until 30th June 2002. Voucher cannot be exchanged for cash or any other merchandise.

---

0 7459.3510 9

£2 off *Unlocking*

This 'Get Caught Reading...the **Word**' voucher £2 is redeemable against the purchase of *Unlocking (BRF)* in all bookshops participating in the promotion. Offer valid until 30th June 2002. Voucher cannot be exchanged for cash or any other merchandise.

---

1 8534.5201 7

£2 off *Christ Empowered Living*

This 'Get Caught Reading...the **Word**' voucher £2 is redeemable against the purchase of *Christ Empowered Living (CWR)* in all bookshops participating in the promotion. Offer valid until 30th June 2002. Voucher cannot be exchanged for cash or any other merchandise.

Get Caught Reading...

the **Word** vouchers

£2 off *Live Like A Jesus Freak*

This 'Get Caught Reading...the **Word**' voucher £2 is redeemable against the purchase of *Live Like A Jesus Freak (Eagle)* in all bookshops participating in the promotion. Offer valid until 30th June 2002. Voucher cannot be exchanged for cash or any other merchandise.

0 8634.7501 9

£2 off *Shannon*

This 'Get Caught Reading...the **Word**' voucher £2 is redeemable against the purchase of *Shannon (Hodder & Stoughton)* in all bookshops participating in the promotion. Offer valid until 30th June 2002. Voucher cannot be exchanged for cash or any other merchandise.

0 3407.8648 5

£2 off *Getting Anger Under Control*

This 'Get Caught Reading...the **Word**' voucher £2 is redeemable against the purchase of *Getting Anger Under Control (Harvest House)* in all bookshops participating in the promotion. Offer valid until 30th June 2002. Voucher cannot be exchanged for cash or any other merchandise.

0 7369.0349 6

£2 off *Travels With A Primate*

This 'Get Caught Reading...the **Word**' voucher £2 is redeemable against the purchase of *Travels With A Primate (HarperCollins)* in all bookshops participating in the promotion. Offer valid until 30th June 2002. Voucher cannot be exchanged for cash or any other merchandise.

0 0071.0633 5

World

WBDVOU33

Please Complete your name & address
Title: Miss/Mr/Mrs/Ms _____
Name _____
Address _____
_____
_____
Postcode _____
email _____

If you would prefer not to receive mailings from the
participating Christian bookshop, publisher or
Send the Light Ltd divisions please tick the box ☐

To the Retailer:
Please accept this voucher as a discount
payment. Vouchers will be credited less normal
discount. This voucher must be returned to:
STL Customer Services
PO Box 300
Carlisle, Cumbria, CA3 0QS
by 31 July 2002.

Name of Shop _____

STL Account No. _____

Cash value 0.0001p

WBDVOU34

Please Complete your name & address
Title: Miss/Mr/Mrs/Ms _____
Name _____
Address _____
_____
_____
Postcode _____
email _____

If you would prefer not to receive mailings from the
participating Christian bookshop, publisher or
Send the Light Ltd divisions please tick the box ☐

To the Retailer:
Please accept this voucher as a discount
payment. Vouchers will be credited less normal
discount. This voucher must be returned to:
STL Customer Services
PO Box 300
Carlisle, Cumbria, CA3 0QS
by 31 July 2002.

Name of Shop _____

STL Account No. _____

Cash value 0.0001p

WBDVOU35

Please Complete your name & address
Title: Miss/Mr/Mrs/Ms _____
Name _____
Address _____
_____
_____
Postcode _____
email _____

If you would prefer not to receive mailings from the
participating Christian bookshop, publisher or
Send the Light Ltd divisions please tick the box ☐

To the Retailer:
Please accept this voucher as a discount
payment. Vouchers will be credited less normal
discount. This voucher must be returned to:
STL Customer Services
PO Box 300
Carlisle, Cumbria, CA3 0QS
by 31 July 2002.

Name of Shop _____

STL Account No. _____

Cash value 0.0001p

WBDVOU36

Please Complete your name & address
Title: Miss/Mr/Mrs/Ms _____
Name _____
Address _____
_____
_____
Postcode _____
email _____

If you would prefer not to receive mailings from the
participating Christian bookshop, publisher or
Send the Light Ltd divisions please tick the box ☐

To the Retailer:
Please accept this voucher as a discount
payment. Vouchers will be credited less normal
discount. This voucher must be returned to:
STL Customer Services
PO Box 300
Carlisle, Cumbria, CA3 0QS
by 31 July 2002.

Name of Shop _____

STL Account No. _____

Cash value 0.0001p

Get Caught Reading…
the Word

vouchers

0 8511.1485 7

£2 off *Incomparable Christ*

This 'Get Caught Reading…the **Word**' voucher £2 is redeemable against the purchase of *Incomparable Christ (IVP)* in all bookshops participating in the promotion. Offer valid until 30th June 2002. Voucher cannot be exchanged for cash or any other merchandise.

---

1 8400.3735 0

£5 off *Behind The Songs*

This 'Get Caught Reading…the **Word**' voucher £5 is redeemable against the purchase of *Behind The Songs (Kevin Mayhew)* in all bookshops participating in the promotion. Offer valid until 30th June 2002. Voucher cannot be exchanged for cash or any other merchandise.

0 8547.6995 1

£1 off *Unquenchable Worshipper*

This 'Get Caught Reading…the **Word**' voucher £1 is redeemable against the purchase of *Unquenchable Worshipper (Kingsway)* in all bookshops participating in the promotion. Offer valid until 30th June 2002. Voucher cannot be exchanged for cash or any other merchandise.

---

1 8542.4520 1

£2 off *Living On Purpose*

This 'Get Caught Reading…the **Word**' voucher £2 is redeemable against the purchase of *Living On Purpose (Monarch)* in all bookshops participating in the promotion. Offer valid until 30th June 2002. Voucher cannot be exchanged for cash or any other merchandise.

0 8024.7296 6

£2 off *Lies Women Believe*

This 'Get Caught Reading…the **Word**' voucher £2 is redeemable against the purchase of *Lies Women Believe (Moody Press)* in all bookshops participating in the promotion. Offer valid until 30th June 2002. Voucher cannot be exchanged for cash or any other merchandise.

---

0 2810.5299 9

£2 off *Mark For Everyone*

This 'Get Caught Reading…the **Word**' voucher £2 is redeemable against the purchase of *Mark For Everyone (SPCK)* in all bookshops participating in the promotion. Offer valid until 30th June 2002. Voucher cannot be exchanged for cash or any other merchandise.

---

1 8599.9503 9

£2 off *Thank God It's Monday*

This 'Get Caught Reading…the **Word**' voucher £2 is redeemable against the purchase of *Thank God It's Monday (Scripture Union)* in all bookshops participating in the promotion. Offer valid until 30th June 2002. Voucher cannot be exchanged for cash or any other merchandise.

---

0 8423.6929 5

£2 off *Bringing Up Boys*

This 'Get Caught Reading…the **Word**' voucher £2 is redeemable against the purchase of *Bringing Up Boys (Tyndale)* in all bookshops participating in the promotion. Offer valid until 30th June 2002. Voucher cannot be exchanged for cash or any other merchandise.

---

0 0071.0766 8

£2 off *Nothing Like A Dame*

This 'Get Caught Reading…the **Word**' voucher £2 is redeemable against the purchase of *Nothing Like A Dame (Zondervan)* in all bookshops participating in the promotion. Offer valid until 30th June 2002. Voucher cannot be exchanged for cash or any other merchandise.

WBDVOU41

Please Complete your name & address
Title: Miss/Mr/Mrs/Ms _____
Name _____
Address _____
_____
_____
Postcode_____
email _____
If you would prefer not to receive mailings from the
participating Christian bookshop, publisher or
Send the Light Ltd divisions please tick the box ☐

To the Retailer:
Please accept this voucher as a discount
payment. Vouchers will be credited less normal
discount. This voucher must be returned to:
STL Customer Services
PO Box 300
Carlisle, Cumbria, CA3 0QS
by 31 July 2002.

Name of Shop _____

STL Account No. _____

Cash value 0.0001p

WBDVOU42

Please Complete your name & address
Title: Miss/Mr/Mrs/Ms _____
Name _____
Address _____
_____
_____
Postcode_____
email _____
If you would prefer not to receive mailings from the
participating Christian bookshop, publisher or
Send the Light Ltd divisions please tick the box ☐

To the Retailer:
Please accept this voucher as a discount
payment. Vouchers will be credited less normal
discount. This voucher must be returned to:
STL Customer Services
PO Box 300
Carlisle, Cumbria, CA3 0QS
by 31 July 2002.

Name of Shop _____

STL Account No. _____

Cash value 0.0001p

WBDVOU43

Please Complete your name & address
Title: Miss/Mr/Mrs/Ms _____
Name _____
Address _____
_____
_____
Postcode_____
email _____
If you would prefer not to receive mailings from the
participating Christian bookshop, publisher or
Send the Light Ltd divisions please tick the box ☐

To the Retailer:
Please accept this voucher as a discount
payment. Vouchers will be credited less normal
discount. This voucher must be returned to:
STL Customer Services
PO Box 300
Carlisle, Cumbria, CA3 0QS
by 31 July 2002.

Name of Shop _____

STL Account No. _____

Cash value 0.0001p

WBDVOU44

Please Complete your name & address
Title: Miss/Mr/Mrs/Ms _____
Name _____
Address _____
_____
_____
Postcode_____
email _____
If you would prefer not to receive mailings from the
participating Christian bookshop, publisher or
Send the Light Ltd divisions please tick the box ☐

To the Retailer:
Please accept this voucher as a discount
payment. Vouchers will be credited less normal
discount. This voucher must be returned to:
STL Customer Services
PO Box 300
Carlisle, Cumbria, CA3 0QS
by 31 July 2002.

Name of Shop _____

STL Account No. _____

Cash value 0.0001p

WBDVOU45

Please Complete your name & address
Title: Miss/Mr/Mrs/Ms _____
Name _____
Address _____
_____
_____
Postcode_____
email _____
If you would prefer not to receive mailings from the
participating Christian bookshop, publisher or
Send the Light Ltd divisions please tick the box ☐

To the Retailer:
Please accept this voucher as a discount
payment. Vouchers will be credited less normal
discount. This voucher must be returned to:
STL Customer Services
PO Box 300
Carlisle, Cumbria, CA3 0QS
by 31 July 2002.

Name of Shop _____

STL Account No. _____

Cash value 0.0001p